THE ULTIMATE

RENT *To* RENT

2-In-1 Book Compilation!

First Printed in Great Britain by
Obex Publishing Ltd in 2020

2 4 6 8 10 9 7 5 3 1

ISBN 978-1-913454-19-7

A CIP catalogue record for this book is available from the
British Library

Obex Publishing Limited
Reg. No. 12169917

CONTENTS

PROPERTY INVESTMENT SECRETS

RENT

TO

RENT

A COMPLETE RENTAL PROPERTY INVESTING GUIDE

SAM WELLMAN

Introduction

Congratulations on your purchase of Property Investment Secrets - Rent to Rent: A Complete Property Investing Guide. You've just made the first move in establishing a rent-to-rent business that will pay off for a long while to come. Purchasing this book is the first step to success - it shows you are willing to learn and ready to take action. You may have already read my second book "Property Investment Secrets – Rent to Rent: You've Got Questions, I've Got Answers!" however this book is laid out as a step by step walkthrough guide, which follows the KISS principle that keeps things straightforward to understand. After reading this guide, you may have some burning questions or just need more information. If that's the case I recommend you check out my second Rent-to-Rent book which addresses everything you could possibly need to know!

Most people already know that buy to let investing strategy can yield great returns, and therefore they appreciate the fundamentals behind the buy to let business model.

The rent-to-rent model has become increasingly more popular in the last few years, mainly because you can get started with little to no investment. In most cases, the most you can expect to invest is one month's rent upfront and the cost of renovation. As your negotiation skills improve, you will see that it is very easy to get landlords to agree to no deposits in return for a long term guaranteed rental agreement.

With regards to renovation, we are not talking about finding a run-down property that needs a new kitchen and bathroom and possibly damp proofing. What you need to remember is you will not own the property, ever. It is in your best interest to find somewhere with minimal work to do. However, if you want to use one of the strategies discussed in this book, there are several requirements and changes that you may need to make to the property. I will cover all of this later, don't worry.

In 2014, I paid £1,500 for a two-day property course in London. I had no money at the time, so this type of investment would seem ridiculous to most people, so I kept it quiet. I had been spending most of my time researching ways to make a passive income, and property investing always seemed to top every list I came across, so I decided to take action.

I felt that 90% of the course was filled with completely useless information to me at the time because I had no money to invest. I made lots of notes throughout, knowing that one day they should be beneficial. In the afternoon during the 2nd day of the course, after I had started to question why I had spent such a large sum of money on this training, the rent-to-rent strategy was discussed. It changed my life as I then realised that £1,500 was soon becoming the best investment I have ever made. Throughout this book I will be providing you with everything I learned that day about the rent-to-rent model, and everything else I have learned since!

As you're about to learn, rent-to-rent can be a quick way to grow money, but it's by no means a "set-it-and-forget-it" business. Rent-to-rent will take your time and effort to understand and implement legitimately. Still, if you digest the lessons and expertise in this book, you'll be able to act fast and grow strong within your first 12 months. When executed correctly, you can expect between £400-£1200 monthly income for each property, and this shows that it is not too difficult to replace your job with your rent-to-rent income.

Inside this book, you'll find what is essentially my crash course on building a rent-to-rent business. You'll learn my secrets and mistakes so that your growth will be even more successful than mine. You will become familiar with the definition of rent-to-rent and what it takes for you to succeed. You will have an appreciation of the risks and benefits associated with the business and how to select the right sublet model and business structure to get you off the ground with little to no start-up capital. I'll teach you what you need to know, and what you need to do to be an ethical rent-to-rent professional, instead of an untrustworthy charmer with a quickly dissolving business.

This book aims to give you everything you need, from contracts to regulations and codes, so that you can run a respectable business that cultivates excellence and supporting the communities you rent to. You'll find there are a good number of individuals that come into this business with no intention of following the rules and representing the profession with honour. If this is your plan, this book is not for you. But if you want to be a well-founded and lawful authority in the world of rent-to-rent and beyond, you're education starts here.

By the time you have completed this book, you should have learned the essentials of creating an ethical rent-to-rent business, with a well-thought-out business plan. You will have selected a business structure that suits you and understood the importance of following GDPR compliance in your business. The simple 5-step process to find the perfect location and the perfect properties to manage will be essential to you. In addition, there is guidance on how to negotiate with property owners; how to complete a successful showing of the property you manage; how to pre-screen tenants and how to secure the final contract. Upon completion, you will know exactly what must happen next to take your business to the next level and develop an ongoing route to achieve maximum success in the rent-to-rent arena.

"What is rent-to-rent?"

Whether you've had experience in real estate or you're brand new to it, you may have heard the term "rent to own" or "rent to buy" in which a tenant rents out a property as their residence, with the intention to buy it from the property owner. The term "rent to rent" is a supplement to that, and it's exactly what it sounds like. An individual rents out a property from a landlord, with the intent to then rent it back out to others. In this case, the individual (the renter) most often does not live at that residence, and it's intended that a third-party (the subletter) will reside in the property instead.

Rent-to-rent is sometimes referred to as "guaranteed rent" because, in the vast majority of these agreements, the renter agrees to pay the property owner a guaranteed and fixed cost each month regardless of whether the subletter has paid all, some, or none of the monthly rent. In fact, even during periods where no subletter resides at the property, like the period of time in-between subletters moving in and out, the renter still pays the property owner a guaranteed rent. This is one of the major benefits that tempts a property owner to such an agreement.

In addition to guaranteed rent, most sublet agreements state that the renter also assumes property management and all of the work and cost that comes with it. These are the two main benefits that make a rent-to-rent offer so appealing to property owners.

"Isn't Subletting illegal?"

Depending on who you ask, you may have heard that subletting is legal, or you may have heard the opposite. In truth, subletting a property is 100% legal- so long as you follow the rules. There are two cardinal rules that ensure your rent-to-rent operation is legitimate.

First, you must have permission from the property owner to conduct a sublet scenario within the property. Some less legitimate people think if the landlord didn't specifically say no subletting is allowed, then it's allowed. Not true. You must have written consent from the property owner, within your contract, to manage a sublet legally. You've heard the expression, "It's easier to ask for forgiveness than permission", but in this case that statement is most definitely incorrect. Asking for forgiveness after conducting an illegal sublet is much more damaging to both you and the property owner (and the subletter) and consequently, the legal implications are much greater.

In some cases, the property owner may not own the property outright, but rather, pays a mortgage on the property. Some lenders state specifically that a mortgaged property is not allowed to engage in subletting, as it puts a considerably higher amount of stress and wear-and-tear on a property when there's frequent resident turnover. In other cases, the insurance company that covers the property may have a similar stipulation against subletting. In both cases, if these terms are compromised, the property owner risks losing the property insurance or the property mortgage (or both). This doesn't end up being just the property owner's problem; it's yours too, as you are the organiser of the sublet.

The second cardinal rule is that your contracts must be bona fide contracts. When you come to an agreement with the property owner, this contract should not be the standard type of rental agreement, but rather, should make clear and specific terms and conditions concerning the sublet operation. As you move through these chapters, you'll see that there are several other rules you need to follow when it comes to running a legal rent-to-rent business, but these two are the most crucial, and really, the foundations to the sublet operation as a whole.

"Is this book right for me?"

This book is for you if...

You've ever been curious about what it takes to start a rent-to-rent business. At some point in your experience, you may have heard that subletting rental properties was a great way to make money quickly. Perhaps you want to explore exactly what's involved in starting that venture, but you'd rather find out from someone who's done it than find out first hand and risk significant failure. You're probably smarter than the average Joe, and you know it can't be so easy. No business worth developing is ever a piece of cake. You're right, and if you keep reading, you'll find that is exactly the case in each of these sections.

You're a brand new rent-to-rent business, but you're not quite sure if you're established properly, following the rules, or setting the strategies that will help you to succeed. If you find yourself in this predicament, you are certainly not alone. If you don't know exactly where you are in the process, or worse still is when you don't have a process, the techniques and instructions in this book can help you identify where you are and where you'd like to be. These lessons will give you the steps to get from here to there.

You're already an established rent-to-rent business but the process isn't moving as quickly as you'd like. It's possible that some of your processes need an overhaul or refinement. It could be that you're aiming too high and are over-ambitious. It could be because you lack the confidence to make the important business decisions. This book will stop the self-doubt and give you the confidence you need to take the next steps to collect your next rental payment.

You've been established a year or more but need to sharpen your aim and update your game. It's easy to get so busy that you forget to grow and develop yourself and seek out new opportunities that will advance your business. Use the information in this book to hone your skills and pull in new prospects and profits from places you forgot to look.

Or maybe you've read my other book "Property Investment Secrets – Rent to Rent: You've Got Questions, I've Got Answers!" and loved it, but wanted a step by step guide!

"How should I use this book for my business?"

With this book, it is my intention to walk you through the simple and the complex of creating a rent-to-rent business. The book is structured to give you an overview of general ideas and then dive more deeply into these ideas as you move through each section. The sections contain facts, experiences, and instructions to help you understand why each part of the overall process is so important and so crucial to making money. You will benefit most if you read this book cover to cover and then return to it often for reminders, techniques and guidance. This book is meant to be used as a field guide and on-going source of reference. Use this as you would use a text from any classroom. Cheat from it, steal from it, and make these techniques your own. Learn from it and come back to leave notes in the margin about how you've improved upon what I've taught you.

Chapter 1:
Orientation to Subletting

You've essentially found yourself at the start of a crash course on making money with subletting. If you're here, there's a high probability that your number one priority is making a profit quickly, and with the least amount of effort and work. Most probably, the idea of investing very little of your own money in order to start turning a significant profit is very appealing.

The idea of generating a small portfolio of rentals from which to make monthly recurring revenue is tantalising. The dream of quitting your job and doing rentals full time seems suddenly so close. It is close; it can be yours. You can manage a small portfolio of rent-to-rent properties that make you a fine supplemental income or even replace the income you're earning now. But you cannot be messy and lazy about the management of it. Do not think that this is an effortless income. As you will see, it does require a fair amount of your time and energy if you are to be successful.

To begin, we'll define key aspects of subletting and identify three of the most popular models used in rent-to-rent business regularly. You'll become acquainted, if you're not already, with what it means to manage rent-to-rent contracts. From what it takes, to what it pays, and all the legalities, formalities, and nitty-gritty work in between. We'll look at the pros and cons of rent-to-rent operations, and strategies you can put in place to ensure you profit quickly and cleanly.

Rent-to-rent is usually not the end goal; it's not the last stop. Most often, it's the first step in generating enough profit to use for bigger and better investment opportunities. As with anything, there are both positive and negative aspects of managing rent-to-rent properties, and we'll examine both.

The information in this section is meant to focus your attention and give you a bird's eye perspective on the overall business of operating rent-to-rent properties. Throughout this crash course, I hope to illustrate to you the lay of the land, the boundaries, and a glimpse of the lands beyond subletting.

Defining Rent-to-Rent and its Main Characters

Let's start at the very beginning and give meaning to the term "rent-to-rent". When we talk about rent-to-rent opportunities, what's meant is subletting. Subletting is the practice of leasing a property from a landlord or property owner, and then renting that unit out to another party for a higher price.

To keep it simple, there are three major players in a sublet scenario:

The Property Owner - This is the person with exclusive rights and control over the property you rent; the lessor

The Renter - That's you, the person renting from the property owner; the lessee.

The Subletter - The third party that rents the property from you at a higher price; the actual occupants of the property.

Local Authorities - In my experience, it helps to consider the fourth party however, since their influence is so great: authorities. This includes both national and local enforcers of housing regulation. It generally also includes any type of business law and regulation you may need to legitimately start your business. It's critical to count local authorities as key players in your business because the impacts are always going to be there and rather than try to go around and avoid them, it ends up being smarter, safer, and faster, in the long run, to approach these head-on. Consider it just another step necessary to successful subletting.

How It Works

It starts with a sublet agreement between you and the property owner. The agreement says that it's permissible for you to sublet your rented space to a third party in your stead. You'd naturally be able to do so because the property would not be your own residence, or you'd often not be at the location for longer periods of time (think travel, school, etc).

Next, an agreement is made between you and the third party to rent the property at a higher cost than that which you pay to the property owner. This, of course, gives you the opportunity to make a profit on the management of the property. This is great for the subletter because they have a well-managed place to reside. It's great for the property owner because they receive a monthly income they can depend on. It's great for you, obviously, for the profit.

In most cases, however, managing the property instead of the owner, and subletting to another party in your place, comes with a handful of responsibility you need to be aware of and prepared for. More than likely, most landlords will be sceptical when you approach them with an offer. This means that you need to have a couple of attractive factors to get a deal that seems good for both parties.

Of course, this comes down to the art of negotiation, but I always tell landlords that all maintenance and general repairs will be upheld by myself. These include general decoration duties and any damage to small items. Structural issues and large repairs, such as window replacement or central heating, will be covered by the property owner. It is essential that this is crystal clear within your contracts.

Another sweetener is to offer the landlord a guaranteed rent for up to 5 years. Of course, I normally start with 2 years, and try to push for no more than a 3-year deal – however when I started, I was so keen to get a property deal I signed a 5-year agreement, but managed to reduce rental payments by £375 a month.

You may be asking yourself why would any landlord ever agree to this, and the answer is simple. As long as you cover the cost of their mortgage payments (if they have one) then they are a having their house paid for without any hassle, without any issues from tenants, without any periods with their house being vacant, and without any agency fees. In addition, in most cases, the property is also increasing in value often over and above the cost of inflation. These are just some of the reasons you can give to the landlord when they express their concerns, or preferably before they even get any doubt in their minds- in your original pitch.

Most importantly, if your subtenant fails to pay you rent on time, you're still responsible for ensuring the owner is paid on time.

Risks of Subletting

For a more comprehensive understanding of how rent-to-rent businesses work, next, we'll take a look at the risks and benefits that come with your new enterprise. Rent-to-rent is not for everyone, and it's critical you assess these factors before deciding to pursue business in this niche.

You're on the Line for Guaranteed Rent

While there are benefits to not owning the property, there are some very important risks to be aware of. Perhaps the most important, which I've mentioned briefly, is the obligation of ensuring your property owner is paid a guaranteed rent each month, regardless of whether your subletter pays (or pays on time). We'll take a look at this in greater detail in a later section and focus on the importance of screening your sublet prospects carefully and cautiously to ensure you're forming an agreement with a tenant that has a reliable history of paying rent on time. Taking accountability for this obligation is an important aspect of the agreement you make with your property owner. It's a big benefit to the owner and thus will act as a key point of leverage for you in coming to a sublet agreement.

Property Maintenance is on Your Tab

Another big benefit to the property owner, and thus another key piece of leverage in your sublet agreement, is relinquishing property management to you, both in terms of financial obligation and effort. In most cases, when you sublet, the upkeep and maintenance for the property is your cost. This is another crucial reason that screening subletters very well is very important.

You Pay Between Tenancy Gaps

For the property owner, this is a big benefit; for you, it's a risk you must plan for. When tenants move out, the property owner usually needs a month or more to handle cleaning and repairs before a new tenant can be signed for the accommodation. In the meantime, the property owner loses that monthly income. But with you subletting the property, the owner is guaranteed not to lose any monthly income between tenants. You'll be paying regardless. So this means you need to do a bit of work upfront to make sure you collect enough to pay rent to the owner during that eventuality. It also means you need to plan for a fast clean up and you need to get a new subletter into the space quickly. For this reason, rent-to-rent businesses should not wait until the month of the move-out to start making new plans. Have a tenant lined up and get cleaning and repairs done quickly (think: within a week).

No Capital Growth

Since you don't own anything in this scenario, it means you don't benefit from capital growth. Over time, the property will (usually) increase in value over time. Capital growth is a huge benefit to owning the property, but it doesn't mean anything to you. This is often why rent-to-rent businesses eventually use the profit they've generated through subletting to invest in a property they can own. This risk, however, does have a silver lining. If the property suffers a loss of value over time, you aren't affected.

Benefits of Subletting

You've Got the Upper Hand on Agents

A property owner seeking to rent out their property might initially turn to an agent for help acquiring legitimate tenants, but this isn't free for the owner and it doesn't address other ownership concerns like guaranteed rent and repair costs. Agents don't help with this, they simply market the property and screen prospective tenants. You, on the other hand, would typically agree to rental payment during gaps and property upkeep. This puts your offer ahead of the agent offer as it benefits the owner in bigger ways. For the owner, accepting a lower guaranteed rental cost from you in exchange for these benefits is often a much more cost-effective solution than paying an agent.

You Set the Rental Price

So you've found a property and an owner to work with you on subletting. If you're a good negotiator, you've been able to convince the owner to charge you a little less than what he or she would normally charge on the market. This can be a very attractive offer for the owner because, in exchange, you'll pay during gaps, manage the tenants, and take care of repairs and cleaning as needed. The benefit for you is that you pay a bit lower of a cost to the landlord each month and you can charge what you like, so long as it's in the range of market prices for the location. This offers you the opportunity to collect the most profit you can each month from the subletter after you've paid the owner your agreed-upon price.

No Stamp Duty or Property Conveyancing Costs

Another benefit of *not* being the property owner is that you're not responsible for Stamp Duty (SDLT), which is a required tax on land and property over £125,000 for residential, and over £150,000 for non-residential properties in England and Northern Ireland. In addition, you'll be able to skip the costly conveyancing process that typically requires a solicitor to finalise transfers and legalities of the property on your behalf. This closing and transfer process is thorough and therefore can take weeks or months to complete, but in a rent-to-rent situation, the finalising of agreements take much less effort and legal regulation and therefore can be wrapped up in several days.

No Mortgages to Secure and Pay

Perhaps the most significant benefit to you is the lack of mortgage work involved. Because you're renting from the property owner, it isn't necessary for you to secure mortgages, which cuts out a significant cost and risk. In many cases, individuals beginning a rent-to-rent business are doing so because they do not have the disposable capital to invest in a mortgage on a property, necessary property updates, and repairs. These same individuals often don't have the credit history necessary for a decent mortgage. In the case of a mortgage, not only are you up against capital and credit, you'll nearly always need a down payment of 20% and sometimes more. Rent-to-rent allows you to skip all this, and go more or less straight to the profit of the business. Accruing income this way allows for a fast and significant profit to be made, which can then be reinvested for more rent-to-rent properties, or perhaps used to establish the capital and credit history needed to branch into property ownership yourself.

Three Basic Sublet Models

As you can see from the benefits and risks of subletting, you don't have as much overall control of the property as the owner has. The owner could essentially decide to forfeit the deal. The owner might not pay the mortgage on the property (assuming there is one) and the property could be repossessed by the lender, leaving you out of pocket and in a sticky spot for recuperating your business loss. Owning a property does give you more control over the entire situation. However, you've likely turned to a rent-to-rent opportunity because you don't have the necessary requirements to mortgage and own the property. So how then, can you set your business to profit as much as possible from a rent-to-rent scenario? There are three basic models for rent-to-rent business that sublet experts rely on to make a generous profit that will help to grow and scale the business. Let's take a look at each so you can decide which model will work best for you. Also, keep in mind that rent-to-rent businesses building a portfolio may choose to sublet properties under each of these models; you don't have to choose just one. To start though, select the model that will be easiest for you to secure and manage, and then grow from there.

1: The Traditional AST Model

The AST model is the most common type of rental in the world of private rentals. AST means Assured Shorthold Tenancy and the lease is typically for 6 months or a year, and then it's subject to renewal. In this model, you rent a property from the owner and sublet the entire unit to one party. With this scenario, you'll negotiate with the owner to pay a lesser guaranteed monthly rent to make a profit from the subletter. This is probably the simplest model for rent-to-rent profit, but you'll need to sharpen those negotiation skills to ensure you're making a profit, especially after tenancy gaps, property management and repairs.

2: The HMO Model and HMO Regulations

An HMO property is a House of Multiple Occupancy. This means you'll have several subletters under one roof. This is not possible with a property suited for only one party, such as a one-bedroom apartment or flat. For each individual you sublet to, you must provide a bedroom; you cannot sublet more than one person to a bedroom. For this reason, if you're planning on subletting one unit to multiple parties, you'll need to find a property that contains multiple bedrooms and at least one receiving room, such as a living room. That said, if you find accommodation with, for example, three bedrooms which have always been rented to one family, you stand to make more profit by renting out each room to a separate tenant. At first glance, it may seem that an HMO unit may not be as desirable on the market but do carry out your due diligence. There are many situations in which prospective tenants find themselves benefitting from a shared living space like an HMO. If the unit is located near a university or an office and industrial neighbourhood, HMOs can do extremely well. Students and young, single, professionals are perfect prospects for an HMO. It goes without saying, that if you're planning on the HMO sublet model, you'll need to make sure your owner agrees to this as well, but if so, then you stand to make a greater profit. In many cases, one or two subletters can make up the guaranteed rent you'll owe the owner, but the additional tenants make up straight profit for your business.

This potential profit looks sensational, but be realistic. This type of model comes with some extra management you'll be responsible for.

First, you'll need to do a smart job in recruiting your tenants, and this means tenants that will get along amiably and not cause you undue personal stress. The good news is that when you sublet to an individual for an HMO, tenants typically expect to live with others they don't necessarily know and are ready to make general compromises with their flatmates to pay a smaller monthly rent themselves. Younger professionals and students are often already used to this type of living situation and make great tenants, so long as you seek out and sign the responsible ones with a decent rental history and stable financial background.

Second, an HMO rent-to-rent often comes with a slightly higher cost of management in terms of utility costs, repairs, and upkeep. Three or four parties in a space that used to house one party translates to a more aggressive use of the property and more wear-and-tear. More electricity, water and heat is used, and a greater bandwidth of internet access is needed, especially in the case of students and professionals.

Third, you need to make yourself aware of restrictions and regulations for an HMO property. For example, the property owner may be open to the idea of an HMO rental, but the mortgage lender may not be. Be sure to do your homework on what's legal and what, if any, licensing is needed for this type of operation. All of this considered, HMO properties are the most popular type of sublet model because of the additional profit than can be easily captured each month. If you're thorough in your search, you can find existing HMO properties that are currently underperforming and rectify this with updates, better management, and better tenants. This takes away a good deal of the upfront preparations and makes you a profit faster and with less effort. Marketing and screening are always going to be a major factor for you, so when you get to the stage of setting up your business and business model, consider these two factors and work them into your plan as a permanent requirement for yourself.

Fourth, if a property is not already set up to receive multiple occupancies, the cost is on you at the start to convert the unit according to relevant regulations.

There are many regulations and modifications needed to operate an HMO, with unlimited fines for anyone running an HMO illegally. To start with, you will need to obtain an HMO Licence if you have 5 or more tenants in a property, forming two or more separate households, or the tenants share a kitchen, bathroom or toilet. For example, if you have a family of 4, plus a lodger, you will need to obtain a license. If you do not meet the above criteria, you may not need to obtain a license but all other regulations should be met to run your small HMO legally.

Different authorities have different requirements, so it is essential that you contact them to check, but I have included a list of common requirements.

All tenants need to sign an HMO tenancy agreement, and you should keep records of all of your tenant's details.

It is your responsibility to regularly check that all appliances are safe all year round, and repair anything as soon as you are made aware of any issues. Gas certificates will need to be sent into the local authorities annually, and electrical certification needs to be available upon request.

Smoke alarms need to be hard-wired in by an electrician on each floor, and you should also have carbon monoxide alarms fitted. You also need to make sure that all bedroom and kitchen doors are self-closing fire doors. Bedroom doors and external doors should have external key locks, with internal thumb turn locks, so in the case of a fire they can easily be unlocked for a quick evacuation. There should also be a fire notice board located in a communal area, such as the kitchen, with a clear evacuation plan for the tenants.

It is also good practice to include a cupboard and fridge/freezer organisation chart on the communal notice board. A good way to do this is to number every bedroom and then have parts of the fridge/freezer separated for each tenant, with a diagram indication which part belongs to each number. You can then put numbers on different cupboards and drawers in the kitchen, so every tenant has space for their food, drink and kitchen essentials.

Anyone under the age of 10 must have a room larger than or equal to 4.64 sqm. Anyone over the age of 10 must have a room larger than or equal to 6.51 sqm, and if a room is to be shared by two adults it must be larger than or equal to 10.22 sqm. The general rule is that there must be one bathroom for every four tenants. If you are looking at a four-bedroom property with the potential to convert a dining room into another bedroom, it must have at least two bathrooms.

You should also be obtaining a TV license on behalf of the household, as it is good practice to provide a TV for the communal living room.

3: The Accommodation Model

Though traditionally this has been the least popular model to follow, its popularity is on the rise, especially with the development of Airbnb. The accommodation model can be your biggest profit maker if managed correctly. With this model, you rent a unit from the owner and then set the space for short-term accommodations, much like an Airbnb space or a hotel space. The space is then rented out to other parties for short periods of time, such as days or weeks; perhaps a month. In most cases, accommodation is rented out to holidaymakers and business professionals.

For a model like this to work successfully, there are a few points to keep in mind. First, you should make sure your owner is aware and happy to comply with this type of subletting. This type of arrangement means a much higher turnover of people coming in and out of the property, and this isn't necessarily something an owner would be happy with because of the general risk involved with the property. You might find that those staying in the accommodation don't respect the property and belongings as much as they would if they resided there. Similar to the HMO model, a space rented as accommodation may also violate a lender's mortgage, so check this first and make sure you're on the up and up. If the owner gives you the thumbs up, you're ready to go! Almost. As you might expect, rented accommodation requires the right location. Holidaymakers and business travellers will not be interested in booking a stay at a place that's out of the way from their primary focus. If the property isn't in a popular location with easy access to the city and transportation, it will be difficult to fill.

Because of the nature of an accommodation rental, there's a bit more in the way of service to think about. Accommodation spaces are almost always fully furnished, including general home appliances like microwaves, toasters, coffee makers, and sometimes even washing machines and dryers. Fully furnishing the accommodation is up to you. You'll want to make sure you offer just about every accoutrement a hotel would. This means a comfortable bed and plenty of fresh linen and towels. Your guest should have a well-equipped kitchen and bathroom, and a comfortable living space to relax or work. A desk or worktop is highly recommended, as the bulk of your guests will be professionals travelling. You'll also need to ensure the property is "turned over" properly between guests. Whether you do it yourself or hire a cleaner, the property should be cleaned from top to bottom in every room. Think of what would be expected from a hotel and do that. This is going to require a bit more management than the other two models.

Next, you should consider your marketing strategy. This is going to require a much different approach than the other two models, as well. As the property will be rented on a short-term basis, you'll need to keep your marketing fresh and relevant to avoid gaps between guests. Marketing like this can cost a bit more, so figure this into your budget.

General upkeep and maintenance of the space and its utilities will be another cost that differs a bit from the other two models. As I mentioned, guests of an accommodation space can tend to treat the space more aggressively than if it was their own residence. Build into your plan a regular assessment of the space and quickly fix anything that compromises the value of the space. Dents, windows, carpets, plumbing and electrical work; all of these should be checked as part of the turnover process. Keep the space fresh and inviting. Because there will be a much higher turnover of tenants, maintenance and upkeep may cost a bit more.

In a typical sublet, you're able to screen your prospects. In a short-term accommodation scenario, a background check is not common, and if it is done, it's generally not as thorough as it would be for an AST or HMO tenant. You lose a bit of control this way and take a slightly bigger risk with the legitimacy of your guests. On the other hand, if you get a rowdy or messy guest, they'll be gone soon. As part of the agreement you make with the subletter, you can create stipulations and parameters to mitigate this, such as disallowing the tenant to have overnight guests or disallowing pets.

With all this in mind, there is a very big benefit to subletting an accommodation space: profit. This model can theoretically bring you the most profit the fastest. The expected market cost for accommodations per day or week is generally much higher than the cost per day or week works out to in an AST or HMO scenario. Your prices are now in competition with other local hotels, motels, and bed and breakfast accommodations. This can quickly add up, and so long as you avoid gaps between guests, you can easily make a higher profit. Just remember that you'll incur additional costs furnishing and maintaining the unit between guests so figure this into your plan.

Personal Preparation

Now you've started to get an overview of what's involved in building a rent-to-rent business for yourself, but there's still a way to go yet. Will you be able to make it to the finish line? This isn't the kind of business you can set and walk away from with the expectation that it will operate on its own. You're seeing it does take effort, especially in place of money when you're starting without much (or any) capital. What else is it going to take from you to make this business grow and succeed? Do you have what it takes or can you get it? Now let's take a look at some of the key qualities and traits that will be required of you if you are to launch a rent-to-rent business with a drive to grow.

Time
It should be clear by now that this kind of business is not passive. You'll need to be involved in probably a daily basis in one respect or another. In many cases, time can be the most difficult commodity you sacrifice, especially if your rent-to-rent business is a side business to another job you're already accountable for. This is perhaps the largest personal preparation you'll need to undertake. Particularly at the onset of your business, you'll need to make time to get the business going, plan your strategy and business goals, negotiate, market your unit, and to manage your tenants and space. If you're hoping to grow quickly, you need

additional time to accomplish this with more than one property. You may already be confident in your ability to manage your time properly, but here are a few tips to keep in mind as you begin:

Prioritise what needs to be done first or with utmost urgency. When you're first starting out, there will be a host of business setup steps and these should not be skipped, but some can fall lower on the list. Decide what needs to be done to get the ball rolling legally and work on your expansion and business identity as you go. Once you've completed the steps to setting up your business, you won't have to do those things again, and you'll get a good portion of your time back, which you can then use to complete some of the other, lesser tasks.

Break large tasks into smaller tasks you can accomplish in about an hour or two. All of the steps in front of you can seem daunting, but if you break them into smaller steps they are more manageable throughout your day or your week. For example, there are several steps involved in negotiating, but rather than think about everything you need to do to sign a contract with your property owner, focus on just one step. Find a contract template that suits the situation. That's one. You could theoretically do that in about 20 minutes online on https://www.LawDepot.co.uk. Edit the contract to fit your business model. That's two. It can probably be done in under an hour. Meet with your property owner to go over the final details. That's three. Instead of planning a whole day to take out of your schedule and accomplish this, it may be much easier for you to do one step each day. It may not feel as though you're moving fast enough, but it will be more manageable, less stressful, and you know in your mind each small step brings you that much closer to your goal.

Don't guess at what's next to be done; make yourself a business roadmap. Outline all the steps you need to take to get one subletter into a unit under your rent-to-rent business and mark out on your calendar or diary when you need (or want) them to be completed by. Be easy on yourself and allow for adjustments in the roadmap. When you've completed those steps, make a new or expanded roadmap from which to work next.

Avoid time-wasting activities and individuals when you can. Interruptions are inevitable, but if you see a friend call to chat while you know you should really be completing a business step, let them go to your voicemail and return the call when you can. You'll have to get a bit selfish with your time, and you should not feel guilty about it. These are the practices you need to embrace to accomplish your goals, and ultimately, to be able to spend more time with the ones you love. By branching out and developing your rent-to-rent business, you're ultimately creating a stronger financial foundation for yourself, which will allow you to more easily spend time with those you love in the long run.

Delegate when you can. While you have a relatively small portfolio its quite manageable to do everything yourself. As you grow, it is essential to look for help. Property managers can sometimes be expensive, but you can strike a good relationship with a handyman or tradesperson that you trust, you can offer them a small percentage per room/property they fill, usually 7-11%. You can often find professional virtual assistants to help you on sites like Fiverr.com or Freelancer.com to help with any admin, bookkeeping or advertising and designing tasks. These tasks can usually be completed at a very low rate because many of the freelance workers on these sites are international and work for a lower cost per hour or per job than you might find in your own backyard. Websites can be created on Fiverr.com to a professional standard for as low as £100, depending on your requirements, and a logo for as little as £5. Though these tasks would be outsourced, the quality of the work remains acceptable because these virtual assistants regularly perform these tasks and understand what's expected despite not being local. If even a low monetary compensation is not in your budget, you can often find apps and programs (even free ones) that automate parts of your process for you. For example, if you plan to run an email marketing campaign for your rent-to-rent business, rather than sending out hundreds of emails yourself, set up a free automated email account, such as reply.io and MailChimp, that will send these emails for you at your specified dates and times. Some of these systems can even be programmed to send response emails when you receive interest from prospects. Take time-consuming tasks off of your list and put them onto the lists of robots or other professionals via delegation.

Don't cancel appointments on yourself. When you put a task into your diary, but there's no one else to be accountable to, it's very easy to cancel your appointment. Don't. Think of a time when you may have put into your diary an appointment to go to the gym in the morning. When the alarm goes off, you're still sleepy, and no one is waiting for you to show up, it's pretty easy to turn the alarm off and roll back into your warm bedsheets. Don't allow this to happen with the self-appointments you set for your rent-to-rent business. Though you might not have a direct person to be accountable to other than yourself, there are ways to prompt your own accountability. Search for free apps that help you to stay on task and accountable to yourself, such as Asana or Stickk. Better yet, use social media to find yourself a mastermind group to join for entrepreneurs, or even more specifically, property management entrepreneurs. These kinds of support groups often have accountability processes built in because you're definitely not the only one facing this challenge. If you know you'll have to report back to your mastermind group with the results of the day, you may be more apt to do them.

Take time to rest. This may sound counterproductive, but burnout is a significant problem. At first, it may feel overwhelming with all you need to get done, but do not sacrifice the time you need to rest and recuperate. You will regret it. If you work yourself ragged, you risk burning out and cutting corners, and that's a poor way to start. Schedule some downtime and take it. The list of tasks will still be there for you when you get back, and they'll be much easier (and more fun) to handle when you've given yourself appropriate downtime.

Accountability

If you've made the time, but don't hold yourself accountable, you've still got some personal development to work on if you're to be successful in this endeavour. It's going to be crucial for you to set tasks and goals for yourself and your business and take responsibility for their completion. Even if you delegate tasks to others, you are still the one ultimately responsible for them. This is why it's a good idea to seek out an application that will keep you on task. My favourite accountability tool right now is Asana, and the reason I love it is that it syncs with my calendar and integrates with a number of time management tools, such as TimeDoctor, which tracks how much time I spend working on each task. I can assign tasks and deadlines to myself and others, and it includes a wide variety of task management features. A tool like this will make your business life much easier. I don't have to fumble with paper notes to myself or wonder what I need to do next, because the app tells me every day what's on my to-do list. You can even make your business roadmap inside this tool. Set dates, hold all of your project documentation and links there; it really does everything you need and it's free! Even if this tool isn't your first choice, there's a wide market of them available to select from. Find one and implement it.

Emotional Control

Things aren't always going to go your way and people aren't always going to do what you want, but it's important to keep your composure. This is true in any entrepreneurial path, but since your rent-to-rent business will involve a fair amount of negotiating, you should sharpen this skill now. Your body language is very revealing whether you're aware of it or not. Your posture, gestures, facial expressions, and breathing are all telling others what you're thinking and feeling even if your words aren't saying it. If you're not already familiar with how to use these aspects of yourself to communicate deliberately, then it's worth a brush-up. Though you may not feel confident negotiating and signing your very first deal, you want to give the impression you are. Though you may not feel like an experienced authority on rent-to-rent opportunities at the start, you want to act and sound as if you are. Believe it or not, these methods of communication can make or break your deal. Studies reveal that over fifty percent of an individual's first impression and opinion of another is based on body language and appearance alone. Only about five percent of an individual's impression of another is based on the words and verbal language communicated.

When you interact with prospective property owners and tenants, be cognizant of your posture. Stand straight with your shoulders back. Make eye contact. Smile. When the prospective client nods, you nod. Take notice of whether your shoulders are squarely facing the prospect or whether they are turned away. The same principle goes for the direction your feet are facing. If your shoulders and feet are facing an exit, for example, it gives the subconscious impression that you're looking for a way out; an escape.

Though it may sound strange, well-regulated breathing makes a significant subconscious impression on your prospects as well. Even if you're nervous, practise slow and steady breathing through your nose during your interaction. It's said that the person in the room with the most control is the one with a steady and calm breathing pattern. These practices may not come naturally at first, but give them some practice in other areas of your life. Practice deliberate body communication when you're in line at the market, when you speak to teachers or coaches, or even with your taxi driver. Make an effort to communicate deliberately and to keep cool under pressure.

Beyond your own body and verbal communication, be aware of theirs. Paying attention to the cues of your prospect will give you insight into how they're feeling and what they're thinking and this can help you build a rapport with them, and even anticipate their questions and decisions. For example, when an individual puts a hand to their face or chin in a gesture of consideration or contemplation, it's generally understood (at least subconsciously) that the individual is making an internal decision, or trying to. However, pay attention to the individual's eyes when this is happening. If the individual is looking straight ahead or even at you, there is no consideration happening internally, and their mind is likely already made up, and probably not in your favour. But if the individual is looking downward, a true consideration of your offer is happening internally. It will benefit you to become familiar with the basics of body language communication so that you can gain insight into the emotions and thoughts of your prospect. Utilise deliberate communication for yourself, and be looking for it in others as you move through your interaction.

Resilience and Adaptability

As is the case in many business pursuits, it helps tremendously to be open and flexible to change. Plans change all the time; priorities shift; deadlines change. Sometimes the prospect you were sure of closing gets cold feet at the last moment. You almost have to expect it and be ready to pivot your plan as needed so you will not slow your momentum. If you have your prime candidate lined up, have a backup candidate as well so you can quickly switch directions and go with another choice at a moment's notice. Make a business plan and roadmap for yourself but don't be afraid to adapt it at any time. While you might first think to change your plans is a sign of poor planning on your part, it's not. Holding tight to a rigid plan with no room for change is the weakness. It can actually be a sign of a strong business to change and adapt regularly. It's a demonstration of your drive and mastery to be able to amend plans and bounce back when things change.

Desire to Learn

While you're well on your way to becoming a professional rent-to-rent business owner and you've already learned much, there's always more to learn and improve upon. Is it in your nature to want that continued learning? Here, you're getting a handle on the fundamentals, but if you're planning to run this business for a while yet, and to grow beyond rent-to-rent, there are many other aspects to become proficient in. The fundamentals in this crash course are solid, but it doesn't hurt to learn the same basics from another source. You'll be able to pick up on nuances, different perspectives, and different ways of operating. You may even notice some information repeats across sources; this can be a sign of details or information you don't want to compromise, and instead, build into your process as tried and true methods and ideas. Continuously put yourself in a learning situation. Join free (or paid) webinars online. Take a class or find a mentor. There are plenty of ways to ensure you're always learning, and thus, always drawing new power from learned information.

Passion for Growth

Rent-to-rent is where you start; it's not where you stop. If you truly plan to keep your business alive, you must plan for it to grow. This often means taking your rent-to-rent profit and eventually securing a property you can own and rent out. Though it doesn't always mean going from renter to owner on units.

In some cases, a rent-to-rent business owner doesn't plan to do anything in the way of property ownership. But this doesn't mean stop growing. There are plenty of ways to remain strictly rent-to-rent and still have a passion to grow and thrive. Scaling your business should always be in the business plan, whether your steps to growth are humble or grand.

In this first section, you've already gained a great deal of information on the business of subletting. You understand what rent-to-rent is and who's a part of it. You've examined the primary risks and benefits of starting a rent-to-rent business. It's now becoming clear to you what it will take, personally, to succeed at this type of business. Best of all, you've learned the three basic rental models and how each of these operates.

With all the information you've accrued so far, you should be able to begin making decisions about your business. In the next section, we'll take a look at a few more fundamental lessons and then I'll show you how to start using this information to make a strategy that will get the momentum going toward your enterprise.

Chapter 2:

Setting a Business Foundation

Now you're picking up speed. You've developed your overall understanding of the world of subletting. In this section, we'll begin to dig into the core components of this business. There are a few more basic concepts to cover before we take steps to set up your business for action. It's critical to understand the laws and restrictions of rent-to-rent. Nothing will take you down faster than trying to squeeze by this step. Learn the laws, use them, and follow them. This is one of the cornerstones you cannot do without. This is paramount to protecting yourself and your business.

I'll also help you to select a rental model, to begin with, and show you how to establish your budget and bandwidth for that model. We'll take a look at who uses these models and why it makes a good choice. If you truly have no money to begin, you may want to consider a borrowing plan that fits into your business model and your budget. I've had to take these steps myself to begin, and I'll walk you through my mistakes so you don't make the same ones. When you're finished with this section, we will have built an outline for your 12-month business plan and the annual goals that will keep your business growing at a healthy rate. Let's begin by examining the moral and ethical implications of the rent-to-rent business.

The Ethical Middleman

In the time that rent-to-rent business schemes have grown in popularity, they've also received a growing number of moral and ethical concerns. In this section, I'll reveal to you the four most concerning issues that continue to come up any time rent-to-rent subletting is discussed. These are the major concerns you need to be familiar with. I encourage you to make ethical choices in your business practice. What goes around, comes around.

Subletting Without Landlord Permission or Licencing

One of the biggest ethical concerns with subletting is deception. If you rent accommodation from a landlord or property owner with the intention to sublet, but you don't get the written okay to do so, you're causing a whole host of problems for every party involved, including yourself. If you sublet without permission from the property owner, you run the very real risk of being immediately removed from the process. Not only that, but the poor unfortunate subletter can also be removed. If the property owner does not own the property outright, but rather pays a mortgage, your sublet activity may very well be a violation of the mortgage. You could essentially get the property owner's property taken away from them. If it's not a violation of the mortgage, or there is no mortgage, it could still be a violation of the property owner's insurance, and that still causes for your removal and the subletter's.

Even if the landlord owns the property outright and there's no mortgage to pay, subletting could still be a violation of the insurance property and the policy could be dropped. You'll be lucky if it's only the property owner that comes after you in court. Watch what you tried to build go down in flames.

While subletting on one or two properties may not require a licence for your business, three or more will require it in England and Wales. If you seek to make a substantial profit, chances are you'll need three or more properties to sublet. It's best to get your licence while in the process of business setup, then you won't need to worry about it when you get the ball rolling on properties. Waiting can slow you down and cause you to miss out on a prime opportunity you find. If you try to circumvent these rules, you could be seeing your personal property taken from you in reparation. Be honest and upfront with your property owners and housing authorities. There are plenty of legitimate opportunities out there that won't require shady business. In short, don't even try it. It's not worth the risk.

Renting to Illegal Immigrants

Another shady practise often found in the business of rent-to-rent is subletting to individuals that do not have legal permission to enter or live in the UK. It's an unfortunate issue, but a very real one; more and more individuals enter the UK without first going through the proper channels whether for work, education, a better quality of life, or even asylum. These individuals and families still need a place to live, and it's here that the dishonest business person awaits their prey. A scenario like this looks like an easy benefit to the corrupt rent-to-rent business owner because you can increase the cost of the unit to take advantage of people who are desperate for housing. Furthermore, the illegal immigrant can do little in the way of protecting themselves from fair rent and good management because they have no legal recourse.

This might sound like an excellent way to gain profit without risk to yourself, but consider this: five years in prison and unlimited fines. These are the penalties looking you in the face if you get caught renting to illegal immigrants. So, what defines an illegal rent such as this? Anything that leads you to believe the individual or party does not have permission to enter or stay in the UK or if that permission has expired. Falsified or even incorrect documentation of permission from these individuals is also included. You run the very real risk of facing these penalties if there's any reason to believe your subletter is illegal. In such a situation, don't expect the property owner to take the fall. If you've sublet, even with your landlord's permission, to an illegal immigrant, it is you who will face the civil penalties.

Trustworthy business professionals will always officially check a tenant's right to rent. If you cannot prove that you've taken this step and documented your investigation, you'll almost certainly be fined. For any tenancy starting on or after 2014 (or 2016 in some areas), you'll need to perform this check before finalising your contract and move-in date with your tenants. To investigate this and document your investigation, the housing authorities require that you ask your prospective tenant for original, genuine, documentation and that you save copies of that documentation at least 28 days before the tenancy begins. Even if an adult tenant is not listed on the lease, but still resides at the location, you'll need to check. There are some cases in which you do not need to check, such as providing social housing or accommodations to refugees, but you'll always want to make sure you've got this base covered. For more specific information on these requirements, you can visit https://www.gov.uk and search for "check your tenant's right to rent", or "right to rent check". You'll be brought to various pages that outline in detail what's required, for who, and when. You can even use the site to link to the housing authorities, which provides an online checking tool to help you. If you've taken these steps, but you're still not sure what to do, your safest bet is to contact local authorities to request further guidance. Contact information is also found on this site.

Surging Rent Costs

Profit. Profit. Profit. This is the goal. However, some sublet businesses take advantage of the opportunity to make a profit off of the ever-growing need for housing, especially in London, Bristol, and larger cities. To make a profit, as you're learning, you'll need to charge a higher cost of rent to your subletters than you're paying to your property owner. This is usually done by striking a deal with the property owner for a lower guaranteed rent than the typical market value. Then, you'll generally spike the rent to your subletter slightly to make up for maintenance and management costs. But "slightly" is the keyword. The legitimate rent-to-rent business owner would theoretically investigate the average market value for renting a unit in whichever city or town the property is located in, and then plan to sublet for a cost of something within that general range.

The unprincipled rent-to-rent professional, however, will raise the cost to the subletter by sometimes double or more. At first, you may wonder how it's possible to close deals with such a high cost, but the growing demand for housing leaves many desperate for space and with no other option but to comply with the costly rent or face homelessness. As this happens more and more, especially in populated cities, we see the market value on rental units surging. Rent-to-rent professionals who do this end up contributing to the growing problem of exorbitant rental costs and affect the local economy in a negative way. Though some individuals may be able to accept and absorb a higher rental cost, many cannot and it forces individuals to make less than desirable choices, like applying for social housing, to make ends meet. Average rental costs skyrocket. It's okay to raise the cost a bit, but price fairly and you'll keep tenants longer, and you won't be responsible for one of the plaguing social issues facing city housing today.

Non-Management

If spiralling rent cost isn't bad enough, many of the unscrupulous sublet businesses take a more than passive position and shirk the responsibility to maintain the property. These "slumlord middlemen" neglect repairs, internal and external repairs, utility management, waste and rubbish removal, and generally make the unit and the neighbourhood drop in value. Not to mention the effect it has on your tenant's quality of life. If you're planning on cutting corners and making a habit of unethical business practices, go ahead and plan for a swarm of trouble to follow you around until you straighten out your game and play nice.

The truth is that a respectable profit can be made legitimately and legally, and you don't have to sink so low to do it. For your business to last and grow, play fairly, do your due diligence, manage your clients, and care for your properties. As you're learning, rent-to-rent business is not passive, and it requires your attention and responsibility. It takes effort to manage your property, tenants, and property owners, and that's only after you've taken the time to market yourself and your units effectively. If you're willing to put in the work though, rent-to-rent can be exactly the footing you need to get you cruising in profitable property management.

What Not to Do

In my time working in both rent-to-rent and buy-to-rent capacities, I've seen many mistakes made, and I've made some myself. I will tell you from my own experience that these mistakes will cost you a good deal of time to repair and recover from and in some cases, time loss is not the only disadvantage you face. Next, we'll quickly roll through what *not* to do in your rent-to-rent business. Some of these mistakes are extensions of points we've already covered but they're worth going into detail and repeating. Let's take a look at what to avoid.

Using the Incorrect Agreements

Avoid getting lazy with your agreements. There is not one agreement to rule them all. The terms in each type of agreement are different and stipulate certain allowances and restrictions. It's possible to download and use standard company let agreements, but it's likely that as you get weeks and months into the rental, you'll find numerous points that haven't been clarified in your contract and you'll wish they were. This will result in your needing to get a new agreement signed part-way through the process, and this will not only take your time and effort, but it can also make you appear unprofessional or untrustworthy. Your property owner may become suspicious of this. Worse, the holes in your contract could be spotted by the property manager themselves, and they will require a drawing up of a new contract, or they may try to take advantage of you. The contract between you and your property managers should be clear about whether or not you have permission to sublet, who is responsible for what management and upkeep, who pays for what and when, how long your agreement is, who and how many individuals can occupy the residence, and what kind of work can (or should) be done to the unit.

In most sublet scenarios, the contract you form between you and the property owners will likely not vary too much. However, there will be differences between subletting residential and commercial units. Make sure you're using the correct version. Beyond that, the terms will vary only slightly between you and your property owners for sublets in a simple situation, so you can probably draw up a contract for residential and one for commercial and continue to use the same contracts by making only the basic changes per opportunity if you're starting with only residential, or only commercial, even easier. It's always better to keep it simple at the outset and build on your success as you go.

Contractually, the biggest differences will occur between you and your subletters, especially if you plan to work with more than one sublet model. You cannot use a standard let agreement to cover all models. If you plan on using each model to make a profit, you need to draw up a contract for ASTs, one for HMOs, and one for accommodations. You cannot use a standard AST contract for HMO model, as all of the relevant clauses need to be added to relate to subletting. I highly recommend getting a solicitor to write up your contracts - there are numerous examples online, such as https://www.LawDepot.co.uk, but cutting corners could come back to haunt you. You could always find a contract you could always get a solicitor to read over it and amend it for you if necessary.

In some cases, you may even need a different contract depending upon who you're subletting to. For example, if you and your property owner should so choose to offer social housing, different rules apply. Once you decide on which model(s) you'll use to start your business, which types of properties you're planning to sublet, and to whom, you'll form a small collection of perhaps a half-dozen contracts. Keep these close to hand and pull out the appropriate agreement when you need it. As you grow, you'll refine your process and your agreements and in fact making these revisions should be a part of your 12-month business plan.

Skipping Licencing, Rules, and Business Insurance

I've said it before, and it's worth repeating, *do not* skip the step of legitimising your sublet business. When you set out, you need to register your business. It's highly unsafe for you to start subletting without this both legally and financially. Similarly, you need to ensure your business. If you don't and something negative occurs, it will be your personal assets that are taken.

Depending on where your business operation is located, and where your rental units are located, business rules can vary. It's important to become familiar with the requirements in your area(s) so you know what operations break the rules and how to avoid them. If you are renting an office from which you work, it will be a different set of requirements than if you work from your own residence. You may even be required to pay business rates, and you may qualify for a deduction of business expenses, which is something definitely worth registering your business for.

If you plan to take on others to help you, whether it be an official employee, an agent, or even in some cases a freelancer, there are several related regulations with which to comply. As you might expect, an official employee is going to require a greater amount of upfront work. For this reason, many rent-to-rent professionals hold off on employing others until they're sure the business is stable. For example, adding employees to your business will likely require you to meet minimum wage, ensure the individual has the right to work in the UK, ensure the individual has no criminal record, register as an employer, and ensure you provide all the necessary accommodations to employees such as a pension plan. The official https://www.gov.uk site outlines all of these requirements and provides details on how to go about all of them. If you are planning on employing others, don't wait until the last minute to take these steps. It's often the case that this takes time, especially going back and forth with officials in the start so you should give yourself a solid month or more to establish these requirements.

Lastly, do not skip proper licencing for the type of sublet model you use. While an AST sublet may not require additional licencing, an HMO or accommodation model will, due to the type of residency. For example, housing authorities want to make sure that if you sublet to multiple separate individuals in one unit, you're doing it in a way that's safe for the tenants. When tenants share common areas, you need to follow a strict set of rules; you can't just go converting kitchens into rooms. The licencing of an HMO sublet business is meant to ensure you know what those rules are and that you follow them. In almost every case, it's you the middleman that needs to apply for this licence. Don't just assume it's the property owner's responsibility. If you are found to be operating an HMO sublet without the correct licence, you and possibly even the property owner will be prosecuted. The rules and regulations are quite clear. Follow them. The fines and punishments are too great to ignore this step. Especially in the case of beginning this business with little to no capital, you cannot afford the penalty. Your entire profit, and likely your assets, will be lost to compensate for skipping this step. Beyond that, you could entirely lose your right to operate as a business altogether.

Subletting for the Entire Term of Your Lease

I've made this mistake myself. It's an easy trap to fall into if you're not aware of it. When you sublet, do not write your sublet contract for the same timeframe of the lease you signed with your property owner. You sublet tenancy should be for at least one day less than the agreement you've set with your property owner. Failing to do so can result in an unscrupulous property owner swooping in on your tenant and collecting the rent you've set, but leaving all the work for you.

Neglecting the Terms and Conditions of the Mortgage or Insurance

Earlier, I mentioned the downfalls of this, but it's another worth repeating. Some mortgages, as well as some insurance policies, include stipulations about letting and subletting, mostly because it opens the door for more damage to the property. For example, some mortgages or policies do not allow for subletting as an HMO or restrict the amount of time in which a property can be leased as an AST. Neglecting these rules can very easily result in the property being repossessed or the insurance policy being dropped. Though the mortgage and the insurance policy may be in the name of the property owner, it's still you - the one who takes the sublet action - that's responsible for this neglect. In such a case, now it's not only the housing authority that will come after you, but it's also probably the property owner, too. In every property you lease from a property owner, check thoroughly through the terms and conditions for both the mortgage and the insurance policy. In some cases, rare ones, the property owner may be willing to make a change to a lender or insurance company that offers a looser agreement that will benefit you both.

As a side note, it pretty much goes without saying, you should not violate the terms of your lease with the property owner, as well. If there's a stipulation in your lease that disallows you to sublet, do not sublet. If your lease makes no mention of whether or not you can sublet, ask. Basically, always ask and get it in writing, that your property owner is allowing you to sublet.

Skipping the Right to Rent Background Check

In most every sublet scenario, it's the middleman's responsibility to perform the check to ensure your prospective tenant has the legal right to live in the UK. Letting to an illegal immigrant is a serious offence that can land you substantial fines at best, and criminal conviction with up to five years in prison in the worst case. Either penalty will stop your business dead. Do not forego this step before finalising your sublet agreement.

Determining Your Most Viable Rental Model

Moving forward, it's time to decide which is the most viable rental model for you to begin with. Finances will have a lot to do with this decision. Which model can you afford to begin? Your bandwidth for management will also play a large part in decision-making at this point. HMOs and accommodation units will almost certainly require more work in management, but your profit will almost certainly be more.

For this reason, this is the method that I prefer, and when the workload gets too much to manage, or you want to make your income stream truly passive, you can always hire a property manager. Finally, your decision should take into account your business growth strategy. Will you be sticking with one model for the entire year, or do you plan to take on other models as you grow?

The Financial Decision

One of the benefits that have probably drawn you to the idea of rent-to-rent initially is the idea that you can begin this business with very little capital, and under the right circumstances, none at all. This is very true, but it does take your understanding to select the wisest model to start. If you're starting with little to no money to invest, ASTs are going to be the simplest and least expensive way to begin. It's relatively easy to find properties that are ready to go as an AST rental. So long as your agreement with your property owner is on the up-and-up in terms of subletting, and the mortgage and insurance permit it, it's effort and time you'll need to invest and not money. However, business licencing, business insurance, and other initial setup requirements could cost you, so plan for this in your initial budget. I've already made it perfectly clear that this is not a step you can skip, but this is the time when it's most tempting. If you truly have nothing to start with, consider various types of borrowing. It's possible to use a line of credit, or a small business loan to defray your start-up costs until you're pulling in a profit.

In many cases, if your credit is strong enough, you may even be able to get a line of credit or a loan that offers 0% interest for a period of time (usually 6 months) if you've repaid by then. Six months is ample time to collect enough profit to repay what you borrowed to start your business. Either way, with little start-up capital, an AST model will be the best choice. If other models are what you're aiming for, consider starting with a few AST properties and branching out as you gain momentum and money. It is possible to find units that are ready to go as HMOs or accommodations, but these almost always cost more to manage, not to mention to begin, as they require more licencing.

If you're starting out with some amount of capital, consider if it's enough to start with an HMO, because this is almost certainly where your greatest profit will be made. If you're setting out with a healthy start-up capital, ask yourself why you're turning to rent-to-rent instead of buy-to-rent models. While it's true that rent-to-rent can take some of the pressure off of you, it likely does not outweigh the benefits. Owning to rent is going to place you in more control and it's going to give you capital growth over time; two huge benefits. Not to mention, if you start as the owner, you are in a position to collect a guaranteed rent and pass the work onto a subletter if you so choose.

Even though I do now own multiple Buy to Let properties as well, it is just too easy to make money from the rent to rent model, so I am still always looking to invest in new opportunities. The main reasons for this are the quick turnaround and the fact that I don't need to outlay the capital for a £40,000 deposit or the astronomical fees involved with Buy to Let.

The Management Decision

As mentioned previously, any of these models are going to take work to manage. Your tenants need attention, and your units need care. No matter what, there will be work to do to set up your business initially. The question is, how much time do you have and how much work can you manage? The longer it takes to set up your business, the longer it takes to make a profit, because you can't- what? Skip this step.

If you plan to manage multiple units, you need to compound the amount of time and effort it's going to take. If this will be your only work, that's one thing, but if you have another part-time or full-time obligation, you'll need to be very proficient at time management. You can't afford to neglect the obligations of starting a business and maintaining tenants and properties. One of the most critical points to apply effort and time will be when sublet agreements are coming to an end. If you don't have the time to market, host viewings, and work negotiations, you'll find yourself having to pay guaranteed rent but not collecting any rent yourself. Letting it go for one month might be alright, but more than that and your quarterly profit starts to drop significantly while your costs still remain.

A couple of AST arrangements might be manageable, but consider the work involved in working an HMO with multiple tenants that need your attention. Further, if you've not done a thorough job of aligning tenants under one roof that get along amiably, you might have social drama to contend with and settling that can take additional time. HMOs, as you've seen, also run the possibility of more initial work upfront to ensure your unit is suitable for multiple tenants while still adhering to all local and national law. An accommodation unit can take the most work because you'll be required to turn over guests relatively quickly, and this includes an entire reset of the unit before the next guest arrives. If you don't have the money to delegate this to others, you'll have to do it yourself. If you cut corners and leave your new guest with lacklustre entry, the word soon gets out, and your bookings suffer.

That raises another point. Marketing is a very crucial part of your enterprise. Again, if you cannot delegate this responsibility, it's on you. If you don't make time for marketing, you're going to have a tough time finding subletters and guests for your units.

The time and effort it takes to start and manage a rent-to-rent business (or even a buy-to-rent business for that matter) is one of the most overlooked and neglected facets in the profession. This isn't necessarily even intended but happens when businesses don't take the time to think and plan it out. Jumping into the business and building momentum and profit quickly is enticing, but without proper planning, time and effort, you'll slow to a stop quickly. Time management is easily the biggest showstopper for a new rent-to-rent business. Plan wisely and avoid the sudden stop.

The Growth Decision

Money, time, and effort are important, but your business growth plan may be the most important to consider when selecting a sublet model to start with. This is last on the list because money, time, and effort all play a part in this decision. However, if you start your business without having this plan in place, it will be extremely difficult to measure your results and success. If you don't have an end goal in mind, at least for the year, you'll just be floating in a sea with no destination and no motor to get you there. Honestly, collecting a profit's great, but what real good is it for your business if you're not using it to grow?

It seems rather obvious the more profit you make, with a model like an HMO or accommodation unit, and the faster you make it, the faster you grow, but not if you don't have a plan for growth. It's very common for a professional to begin with a few AST-style properties and as profit comes in and costs are mitigated and defrayed, that profit is invested into an HMO or accommodation unit. It's also very common for that profit to be put toward a buy-to-rent opportunity so that the property's capital growth is yours. Each of these will require more money and more time, especially if you begin to delegate aspects of your obligations.

My advice to you is to run the general numbers and find something that's manageable and easily affordable, even leaving you with room to wiggle. As you get closer to the time when you can expand, and you've got your eye on a few prospective units to help you do so, run the numbers again, this time more specifically. What will it take to invest in a more profitable sublet model and by what point do you expect to start that expansion? Six months? Nine months? A year? Two? There's no wrong answer except not planning. Make a benchmark for yourself and don't hesitate to refine this plan as you go. It's really the only way you'll know if you're on track for growth, and if not, what needs to change to get you back on track. When you have a general outline for growth over 12 months, it will make choosing a sublet model quite easy.

If you've taken these steps and you're still having trouble deciding where to start, start small and simple; start with an

AST model. It will allow you to get the hang of the business quickly and to project the amount of time and money it will require to take on a bigger project like an HMO or accommodation model.

It's worth mentioning at this point that ASTs, HMOs, and accommodation units are not the only models for subletting. Another model you'll find, though less common for a rent-to-rent business is letting to a lodger.

The Lodging Model

Let's assume for a moment that you reside under a common AST model, or even in a home you already own. Let's also assume, too, that you haven't the capital, and maybe even the time, to dedicate to subletting. You still want to make some form of profit. Offering lodging might be a solid temporary solution to get you off the ground and into the world of profitable subletting.

The lodging model is a simple one with few regulations, though the regulations that do exist are still just as important to adhere to. Whether you're a tenant of a landlord's AST property or you own your own home, you still need to ensure your ability to take in a lodger. As a tenant, you need to make sure your landlord will allow you to have a lodger. As an owner, you need to ensure you don't violate mortgage or insurance terms by taking in a lodger.

What's the difference between a lodger and a subletter? Mostly, control. A subletter has a right to their own room, and the landlord (including you) cannot enter without permission. You also cannot dictate (to an extent) how the subletter uses that

room. A lodger, on the other hand, doesn't hold that
control. You can enter a lodger's room as it is essentially still
your room. A lodger must still have access to kitchen and
bathroom facilities within the property, however. There are a
few other stipulations to be familiar with in a lodging situation,
such as offering to lodge to a family member or offering to
lodge in a unit that's already part of social housing. There are
regulations for the income made from a lodging room and the
taxes you're subject to, as well as credits. Lodging, like any of
these models, will require that the entire unit (not just the
room) is up to code, safe, and provides necessary utilities and
accommodations. You'll also still be responsible for a Right to
Rent check. If you're considering a lodging unit as your starting
point, visit https://www.gov.uk for the specifics in your area
and for your specific situation. A lodging model is going to be
the least profitable model to use, but if it's all you can manage,
it might be better than nothing at all. But keep in mind, now
you have to share a space with your lodger and this might
impinge on your own quality of life.

Your 12-Month Business Plan and Annual Growth Goals

Sometimes start-up businesses don't make a 12-month plan at
the outset. Let this be another of my own mistakes you learn
from and avoid. I didn't have a business plan in year one or year
two, and it really slowed my growth. Sure, I was making a
profit, but I was spinning my wheels on where to go next and
burning money on how to get there. I had no orientation on
how to get to what's next because I had no plan. At the end of
the fourth quarter in year two, I decided enough was enough,
and it was time to get serious. I spent most of October and

November building my written business plan for the upcoming 12 months. The success and confidence I experienced in year three was an exceptional difference. Have that exceptional success for yourself in year one. Make a 12-month business plan complete with goals for your business growth.

There are three common types of written business plans:

Working Business Plan - A rough internal document that you work from and share with others inside the business. It's your business guideline, and it's used regularly to steer your ship. This plan is generally very descriptive to help your internal staff and yourself, but it's not necessarily beautiful. It's not necessarily something you'd want to present without formalising it.

Abbreviated Business Plan - Whereas formal business plans can be upwards of twenty pages long; an abbreviated plan is about 1-5 pages in length. It includes most or all of the complete formal version, but typically not as much detail is provided in each section. This version of your business plan is typically used when trying to get help from lenders or investors and the like, so it should be a presentable copy that's clear for all who read it.

A Formal Business Plan - A full and complete business plan ready for any audience you wish to share it with. This version of your business plan can be as long as 10 or 20 pages and includes all the typical sections of a business plan in detail, including financial records and other formal documentation. This can be used for lenders and investors, but keep in mind that sometimes these parties are more interested in the abbreviated plan.

It's hard to compose, and even harder to follow, a 12-month business plan if you're not sure what it is or how to use it. Your business plan should clearly describe your business, its components, its goals, and its plans to reach those goals. A business plan also often includes legal business documentation and financial records, but this is more so the case in abbreviated or formal presentation plans with and external receiving audience.

There's an old idea that a 12-month business strategy is more about the planning and less about the plan. What's meant by that is the process of sitting down to write out the sections of a business plan forces you to think about aspects of your business you may not have considered so that when that part of the plan arrives, or better yet when an unforeseen circumstance arises, you've got a guideline on how to operate and still aim toward your goals.

It's important to remember your 12-month business plan is a living document. Remember when I mentioned adaptability and resilience? The business plan is a perfect example of where to apply that quality, especially at year one. The document will change and grow in order to overcome challenges, obstacles, and shifting goals. It's not a rigid dictation of exactly what must happen or else, and in fact, it's unhealthy for your business to treat it as such.

The major mistake made with a 12-month rent-to-rent business plan is the amount of time and effort put into it. It's often too much or too little time. Keep your audience in mind when making your plan. Will you be showing it to investors or using it internally? The level of time and detail you put into it will be affected by whether the document is meant to be presented or used as a guide internally. While you certainly want to spend more than a day to create your business plan, you probably don't want to spend more than a month making it, or it's taking up too much of your time. If start-up capital isn't a problem for you, you can often find freelance professionals who can draw up your business plan for you. When you make your initial 12-month plan, you want to aim for somewhere between a working plan and an abbreviated plan (unless you plan to seek out investors and the like) and it should be about 3-5 pages in length. Remember to back up your plans with metrics, numbers, and projections.

So what goes into a business plan? A business plan doesn't necessarily need to follow a certain format, but it should include certain information and sections. Let's take a look:

Executive Summary

This is typically at the start of the document, and it includes a description of your rent-to-rent business; the business concept and the mission statement. This part of the document is meant to give those reading it a general understanding of how the business operates. This typically explains the day-to-day business functions, the location and surrounding environment of the business, and the people involved in performing regular tasks for the business.

Financial Status and Strategy

This section of the 12-month business plan can vary a bit depending on whether your business is new and just starting or whether you're several years into the business. If you're new, this section typically includes a breakdown of the start-up costs you anticipate, that business capital you currently have or want to establish, usually through a borrowing plan. This section should also include a projected cash flow statement and a profit-and-loss statement. Great plans will also include a break-even analysis that describes how your business plans to at least break even if no significant profit is made over the course of 12 months. This is more important to include if you seek to borrow money and you're presenting this business plan to lenders or investors.

Marketing Strategy

While this section is often more significant for businesses selling a product, it's still important to include it, though it doesn't have to be as long as a business plan that includes sold products at a brick-and-mortar location or via eCommerce. In this section, you should include a description of how you plan to market your properties online and/or in the community. This could include any social media marketing plans, Google Ads, the viewing and negotiation process, and even networking strategies, which is part of any successful rent-to-rent business.

Customer Analysis

This section of your business plan should include a breakdown of the customer base you intend to serve. Describe your primary customer; your ideal customer; your target customer. If you plan to serve one sort of customer during the start of the year, but you plan to expand or shift to another sort of customer within your 12-month period, explain that as well. If you can, describe your customer's median income and what that customer is used to paying for your services in your area.

Competition Analysis

This section should include a profile of the competition and their services, the amount of competition in your region, and the median cost for their services. Describe what the competition does for marketing, the length of time the average competition has been operational in your region, and probably most importantly, how you plan to compete. Find what sets you apart from the competition and makes your services unique. This will often be the number one way you get a leg up on the competition.

Industry Analysis

Your lenders, investors, and other interested business parties may not always be familiar with the industry or profession in which you work. Describe to them in this section what the industry profile is. Explain what the industry has looked like in your region over the last five years and whether cost and profit have increased or decreased. Include the supply and demand for these industry services and the expected projection for this over the next five years.

SWOT Analysis

Perhaps one of the most important sections for you to complete - for yourself - is a SWOT analysis. A SWOT analysis is a comprehensive study of your business' strengths and weaknesses; your opportunities and threats. Taking time to write up this portion of the business plan is often very revealing and will allow you to spot concerns and opportunities you may not have noticed without performing this bit of work. It's a beneficial section for the audience of your document, but this is almost always more important to the business itself as a planning tool. I highly recommend you concentrate efforts on this section of your 12-month business plan, and perhaps even start here and use what you find to determine other sections of your business strategy.

Contingency Plan

In this section of your document, you need to plan for worst-case scenarios. The contingency plan is used to prepare for an outcome that's unlikely, but disastrous if it should occur. Explain why the outcome would be a huge negative impact on your business. Describe how your business plans to mitigate these damages and repair them, should they occur.

Goals and KPIs

Goals and KPIs (Key Performance Indicators) are often a part of each relevant section, but usually, a 12-month business plan will dedicate an entire section to defining the milestone goals that will determine your success and growth. KPIs and other metrics are used to measure the success of each goal so that you can tell how much under or over your goal your business has performed. It also serves as an excellent gauge on the timeframe in which each of these goals is accomplished so you can tell if your projected timeframe is over, under, or right on target. Year over year, this part of your plan will serve as a crucial element in your growth. You'll be able to compare last year's goals and KPIs with the goals you set for the coming year.

Elevator Pitch

A 12-month business plan does not necessarily require the inclusion of your "elevator pitch", but this is an excellent exercise and inclusion for new businesses. Including a section for your elevator pitch will allow you to focus and refine the explanation of what your business does, in a way that others can understand in about 30 seconds or less.

If you're feeling overwhelmed, putting together a 12-month business plan for the first time, don't panic. Every business owner has been where you are now. It is tricky, but it's possible, and once you start in on the project it becomes easier. Better yet, it opens you up to a perspective on your business and its growth that you may likely not have seen. To make life easier, there are several software applications and business plan templates available online, both for free and for cost, that can help you to make this plan. There are videos online to walk you through the details. If you have the budget for it, there are services that will make your plan for you with your help and then review it with you to make sure you benefit from it as much as your audience will.

It can be overwhelming to draw up a 12-month business plan for the first time, but it's going to be much more difficult for you if you skip this step; take my word for it. Fortunately, your year two business plan will be easier for you. Your business start-up will be complete, so you won't need to cover that additional concept. You'll have already made one plan, so the second will be all the easier to manage. When you get to year two, you can compare your plan with the year one plan. Just think how easy next year's plan will be if you start now.

Chapter 3:

The Business Setup

You've essentially found yourself at the start of a fantastic job thus far! You've made it past the majority of the heavy-lifting concepts. You have a solid grip on which sublet model(s) you're interested in working with and hopefully you've chosen which to begin with first. You're aware of the risks and benefits associated with each and the legal regulations to which you should adhere. You know what a business like this is going to require from you in terms of money, time, effort, and personal characteristics. I've given you the five most common mistakes to avoid when starting your rent-to-rent business so that you can learn from them without making them. Best yet, you've developed an understanding of how to set yourself up with a comprehensive and insightful 12-month business plan to use as your guide through the next year and beyond. Now it's time to dive into the nitty-gritty and focus on the step-by-step actions you need to take to establish your rent-to-rent business so you can get yourself registered as a legal operation.

In this section, I'll help you to select a business structure (not to be confused with your sublet model) and gathering the appropriate documentation and contracts you'll need to conduct business. We'll take a quick look at what it means to become a part of a redress scheme for your business and how to protect the rights of your prospects as you collect personal information from them. We learned earlier that more than fifty percent of an individual's opinion of you is formed by your body language and appearance, and this is not much different for your business. Lastly, I'll run you through the basics of establishing your business locally and online so that it's easy for individuals to find your business, your available properties, and feel confident working with your business because of your professional image. Let's get started.

Select a Business Structure

There are three types of business structures that make sense for you to select from in order to start your small rent-to-rent business. As with anything, there are advantages and disadvantages to each. When you select one structure, it doesn't mean you're stuck with that forever. It's common for a business to start with one structure and to grow into another as your success grows. Let's get into it and see which structure will work best for your year one business.

Sole Trader Business Structure

A sole trader structure is the simplest and fastest to set up, but it carries the most risk. As a sole trader, you're a legal business but set up under your own personal identity. Any financial damage incurred is your personal responsibility to repair with your own financial assets. If another individual, business, or insurance company comes after you legally, it's you personally they come after and there's no way for you to deflect that to your business, since you personally are the business.

Limited Company Structure

A limited company structure allows you to set up your business separate from yourself so that if, heaven forbid, your business starts to head south, you are not personally responsible for these debts. It's a bit more work at the outset and you'll be responsible for following a stricter set of rules, but my personal recommendation is that these additional steps, rules, and costs are well worth it to protect your personal assets. As a limited company, you'll be responsible for formal documentation of company records and for updating any business structure changes you make throughout the year. If you have the budget, it often helps to hire an accountant to help with these additional responsibilities. If that's not in your budget, it's possible to do this yourself, but it will take you some extra time and effort. Fortunately, the internet is full of help and software applications to make this management easier. You'll also be required to file company tax returns and pay corporate taxes. Setting up as a limited company, but then not following these rules can result in fines, prosecution, and even disqualification of your business. Having a Limited Company can also have many tax benefits, especially the fact that the dividends tax bracket is lower than the PAYE income tax bracket, but it's worth speaking to a tax advisor or accountant for more information.

Partnership Structures

If you're starting your rent-to-rent business with at least one other interested party, a partnership structure may be your best choice. A partnership structure is the most complex of the three options, but as you might suspect, the available opportunities may be greater for you depending on your circumstances. It's important to note at this point that a partnership does not necessarily mean two (or more) individuals. A partnership can exist between two (or more) individuals, an individual and an existing limited company, or two (or more) limited companies. That is to say a limited company essentially counts as a 'legal person'.

There are also two different types of partnerships from which to select your structure: a limited partnership, and a limited liability partnership. The major difference between these two partnerships, for our intents at least, is the liability. In a limited partnership, both partners (whether limited company or individual) are personally responsible for debts incurred by the business partnership. However, each partner is personally responsible for debts only up to the amount of which that partner has contributed to the business. In a limited liability partnership, partners are better protected from personal liability.

However, the intricacies of partnership structures are greater. For example, in a limited partnership, one partner must be named the 'general partner' and the other party, or parties, should be listed as limited partners. The limited partner(s) are not able to take on as much business responsibility. A general limited partner is responsible for any debts the business is not able to pay, and they basically control and manage the business. The general partner is able to make binding business decisions, whereas the limited partner is not. The limited partner is only liable for the business debts up to the amount of which they've contributed to the business and they are not able to make as many business decisions, especially binding decisions. Partners split profits and pay taxes independently on what they've collected. Beyond liability and responsibility differences, and declaring general and limited partners, there are a few other things to keep in mind in the case of a partnership business establishment.

A limited partnership must include an official business address. You can use a PO Box address, but you still must register a main physical address from which business is conducted. This can be a home address, but note that this address will be publicly available. Also, note that your official business address must be in the same country that your partnership is registered in.

There are also stipulations as to what your business name can be. You do not have to register an official business name in the case of a limited partnership. You can trade under your own names, but all partner names and the business name (if you have one) must be included on all official documents such as business documentation, business letters, and invoices. A limited partnership establishment must not use terms such as "limited liability partnership" or "LLP", as it is technically not an LLP. Your partnership business name cannot include offensive or socially sensitive terms, and it cannot be the same as an already existing trademark business name. Your business name cannot suggest your connection to government or local authorities and it cannot use the term "accredited". There are some exceptions to these business name rules, but you must receive prior written permission from the Company House in order to do so.

In the case of a limited liability partnership, you must register a business address, and just like a limited partnership, this address can be a PO Box, but you must also register a physical address, and this address must be the same. Again, it can be a home address, but note that this address will be available to the public.

A limited liability partnership does need to have an official name; you cannot trade under your personal identity alone. This business must include the term "limited liability partnership" or "LLP" as part of the name. This business name must be registered with Companies House, the same as a limited partnership should. Same as with a limited partnership, your business name must not suggest or use official terms without written permission and it must not be the same or too close to a similar name of an already existing business unless you have written consent from that entity to use it. If for some reason, you want to operate under a different business name than your official limited liability partnership name, you can, and you need not register that name, but it still needs to follow a few certain rules, such as, it cannot use the term "limited" or "LTD" in that name.

Similarly to the way a limited partnership must determine a general partner and a limited partner, a limited liability partnership must determine at least two "designated partners" which will be responsible for official business documentation, record-keeping, and decision-making. The other partners, should you have any, would be general partners. Designated partners are responsible for registering the business for Self-Assessment with HMRC, and they must also be individually registered for Self-Assessment themselves. If your rent-to-rent partnership plans to make greater than £85,000 a year, a designated partner must register the business for VAT, prepare, sign, and send annual accounts and confirmation statements to Companies House. Since designated members hold accountability, if they fail to comply with business requirements, they are subject to fines and prosecution.

If you make the decision to use a limited liability partnership and establish designated partners, because there must be at least two, it's important to take the extra step of creating an LLP agreement between those designated members in order to be clear about who does what, how profits will be shared, and how partners will join or leave the LLP.

Join the PRS

The PRS, or Property Redress Scheme, is authorised by the Department for Communities and Local Government ("DCLG") and by the National Trading Standards Estate Agency Team to help consumers with complaints and disputes in a rent-to-rent scenario. Since you are a middleman and service, both the property owner and the tenant, your position can be a precarious one, and you are not always the best individual to resolve these issues. If a complaint or dispute is raised to you from either the property owner or the tenant, you should, of course, seek to resolve the issue to your best, and unbiased, ability. However, this is not always an easy task, especially where your own profit is concerned. Instead, unresolved complaints from either the property owner or the tenant can be raised to the PRS for resolution if none has been found. The PRS acts as an independent and unbiased agency, and though the focus is to help the consumer, it's a huge help to you as well. Becoming a member of the PRS shows that your business is dedicated to excellent customer service for both your landlords and tenants. It also suggests that you care deeply about improving property industry standards in your region.

If a complaint is raised to the PRS, the process for resolution is a fairly simple one that is completed within 40 days from the time of the complaint. Members (that would be you) are given the opportunity to resolve the complaint first. If that doesn't work, the PRS acts as a mediator to try to come to a fair agreement for all. And if that doesn't work, the Property Redress Scheme Ombudsman will make a binding decision that all parties must adhere to.

In short, your rent-to-rent business *must* join the PRS, according to the Consumers, Estate Agents, and Redress Act (CEARA) of 2007 (in England). Joining is easy and affordable. To join, you must submit an application which identifies the name of your business, the services you provide, the main point of contact, any additional branches of your business, and the personal details of at least one of your business partners. If you have no partners, it's you. When your application is accepted, you must pay an annual membership fee of £200 or less, depending on the type of membership you seek. When you've paid, the PRS provides a sticker for display at your place of operation, and leaflets which should be given to your clients; both property owners and tenants upon finalising and closing your contracts with each.

If you fail to join the PRS and a complaint is lodged against you, you risk having to submit and pay anyhow, and on top of that you risk fines. This is another step you just *do not* skip if you're operating a respectable, ethical, and legitimate rent-to-rent business. I know you agree that is the goal.

Gather Your Contracts

If your business is now set up, you're ready to start gathering the contracts you'll need in order to officially finalise the terms and conditions you've established with your clients. At this point, we'll assume you've chosen the sublet model that you're going to start your business with. If you're ready to start gathering contracts, you'll need to know if you're using the AST model, the HMO model, or the accommodations model. There are different contracts for each of these models, and even different subgroups of contracts under each of these models depending on a variety of factors, such as whether your property owner owns their property or mortgages it.

You are going to need at least two major contracts to get going: a management contract and a tenancy contract. The management contract is formed between you and the property owner, and the tenancy contract is obviously formed between you and the tenants you sublet to.

The good news is that once you've found template contracts to use for both management and tenancy, you can perform major and necessary edits to the contract once, and you'll likely not need to make these adjustments again for a while. Of course, you'll always need to edit some specific details for every single contract you draw up, but that's to be expected. The details of the terms and conditions will typically stay the same. That's not to say you can't edit the terms and conditions; that's up to you.

The better news is that despite the internet overflowing with property management and tenancy contracts, many trying to be sold, there's actually a wonderful organisation, that I have previously mentioned, that provides PDF versions of these contracts for free. Law Depot https://www.lawdepot.co.uk has been helping individuals and businesses with contracts since 2001, and they've served over 10 million parties in that time. Their library of contracts is extensive and covers not only the contracts you'll need for management and tenancy but anything you need for your business setup as well. They've got an in-house team of legal pros and an excellent, readily available staff to help you. They're easy to contact by phone, email, or even chat. They receive positive reviews and have been suggested as a trustworthy resource by businesses like The Wall Street Journal, Time Magazine, and The Washington Post.

GDPR Compliance

If you're not yet familiar with GDPR compliance, well, where have you been? Have you noticed that for the last year, every site you visit asks you to accept or refuse cookies? That's part of GDPR compliance. A minuscule part actually. GDPR or the General Data Protection Regulation is honestly an enormous concept with hundreds, if not thousands, of facets to it. GDPR deals with the protection, processing, storage, and movement of personal information collected through business and commerce.

If you stop for a moment and think about all of the various kinds of business and commerce that take place every day and all of the possible points in which any personal information is collected to do so, your head will start to swim. Personal information could be a name, a phone number or email address, an IP address, a credit card number; it can even be a business card you collected from someone at a networking event. There are seemingly endless points in a business interaction where personal information is collected. Once the information is collected, it's generally processed in some way and stored somehow, be it in a hardcopy file in your office, or in the digital cloud.

Since 2016, the European Commission has been building the data protection regulation that would replace 1995's Data Protection Directive with clear and stringent rules for collecting, processing, storing, and moving personal data. In May 2018, GDPR compliance was rolled out and implemented, and any business found not complying is subject to hefty fines. Even though the UK plans to leave the European Union, it will still have to comply with GDPR ruling, and so will you. GDPR is easily the single most significant change in the way business is conducted in at least the last 25 years. It's no small concern, and you must be properly attentive to it.

The general idea behind GDPR is for businesses to increase the security and transparency of the personal information they collect. The EU does this by giving the owner of the personal data (the person whose data it is) more control over what happens with their information, and the ability to have that information removed from databases should they no longer wish for the business to possess it.

For you, that means any information you collect from prospects, property owners, tenants, suppliers, employees, or industry colleagues. So how is your rent-to-rent business supposed to handle all of this information in compliance with GDPR legislation? In the grand scheme, GDPR contains a complete eleven (long) chapters outlining all how a business should comply. While you may not need to understand all eleven chapters of this legislation at this point, you should familiarise yourself with what those chapters are in general. This way, as situations arise, you know where to look to make sure you're complying appropriately.

Everything GDPR can be found on the data protection pages of the European Commission, here: https://ec.europa.eu/info/law/law-topic/data-protection_en. The site is remarkably well-managed, current, and easy to use and search. The information on the site comes directly from the European Commission so you can be confident it's accurate and up-to-date information. The eleven chapters deal with the following:

General Provisions

This first section outlines the purposes and definitions of general data protection. This section will tell you that the "data owner" is the individual to whom the data belongs; the person who can be identified in any way at all by the information collected. The "data controller" is the organisation which collects the information. The "data processor" is the organisation that processes the information. The provisions section makes it clear that GDPR compliance is strictly for business and information you may collect personally, like the phone number of a person you'd like to take on a date, is not subject to GDPR compliance. This section will give you a solid understanding of what GDPR is all about.

Principles

This section explains the moral and ethical implications of GDPR compliance; when it is and isn't permissible to collect, process, store, and move personal data. It covers factors about collecting personal information from individuals under legal age, and how long is legally appropriate to store data on individuals. Familiarising with the principles of GDPR is also a great idea because it gives your business an overall idea of the rights and wrongs of compliance, so again, when a situation arises, you have in the back of your mind that you should take a few minutes to investigate and make sure you're complying.

The Rights of the Data Owner

This section outlines and details the new level of control an individual has to dictate what an organisation does with the individual's personal information. For example, if I were to visit a site to download a management contract to use in my rent-to-rent business, the download is generally permitted only after I share my email address with the site. I can in theory, download that form, and then make a written request to the site to delete my personal information; my email address and that organisation must comply. They have a certain amount of time in which to remove my information from their databases, and any other associated database to which they've passed my information. Similarly, if an individual wants to know exactly what information an organisation holds on them, the organisation must comply and provide a complete profile of all the information they hold on that individual. At any time, an individual holds the right to have their information rectified or erased.

Controller and Processor

These sections breakdown and define everything that the controller and the processor must do with the information to comply with GDPR legislation. This includes how and when to process personal information, how to generate appropriate anonymity for parts of collected personal data. For example, when you enter your credit card number online and all numbers are X'ed out except for the last four digits, this is a version of

Pseudonymisation, which is making part of the information unidentifiable for the protection of the individual. This is particularly important as we hear of more and more organisation sites getting hacked and personal information stolen. These sections explain how to officially process and store information and the security that goes along with it. For example, if my business collects personal information from a tenant, I would store that information in a CRM database. But the supplier of that database and their servers must be GDPR-compliant servers, or it is I who violates compliance. It also includes several official resources an organisation may use to better learn about and comply with GDPR.

Liability and Penalties

This section defines the risks of non-compliance by any business organisation. This includes the warning process and the breakdown of fines your business faces should you be found to be non-compliant. It provides an understanding of what legal obligations the controller must adhere to and the consequences of not doing so.

B2B Marketing

GDPR draws a strict line between personal information collected for the purposes of business-to-consumer (B2C) marketing, such as a utility company storing information about its customers, and business-to-business (B2B) marketing, such as an accountant collecting information from the businesses it provides services to. If the world of rent-to-rent, you'll most likely be working in a B2C capacity, unless, for example, the property owner operates a business and it's that business you're actually interacting with when making agreements and contracts.

Restrictions

Final sections of the GDPR legislation cover unusual scenarios that deal with individual data protection. This includes compliance for situations like lawful interception of data, such as in the case of national security, military, police, and the justice system. It also includes collecting and storing of personal data for statistical and scientific purposes, deceased persons, and further restrictions for collecting and storing information on employees and partners.

While again, you probably don't need to be knee-deep in GDPR compliance as you begin your rent-to-rent business, there are a few steps your business should take from the outset to practice compliance. Get familiar with GDPR. Check! You've just done it. You now know where to find more information if you wish to become intimately familiar, as well.

Ensure three major components of GDPR compliance are evident on your business website. This includes making sure your site is secure, which means your website address should begin with "https" and not just "http". Your website should also implement the Cookie banner I mentioned earlier, which makes it obvious to any visitor of your site that your site uses cookies and it allows the visitor to accept or decline the use of cookies with their IP address. Finally, your site should update any opt-in form to comply with GDPR. For example, if you make a purchase online, often times one of the last checkboxes you see is the company asking if you'd like to receive marketing emails in the future from this company. This is compliant. What's not compliant is using the collected personal information to market to the individual in the future without having asked or notified the individual of such. The individual must always be presented with the ability to opt in- or -out of such practices.

With your familiarity and business site covered, the last step you should take is to ensure your suppliers are also compliant. For example, if you use Salesforce.com to store your CRM information, you should make sure that Salesforce.com is also compliant (they are) or your business is in violation, for the pure fact that it's your own responsibility to choose your suppliers carefully.

For every tool, freelancer, or B2B business you work with, you should make sure they comply. Because GDPR is such a big issue, most suppliers provide a page on their own site that explains their level of GDPR compliance. If you scroll to the bottom of most any site, you'll find links to items such as Terms and Conditions, Privacy Policy, and Cookies Preferences. If you visit these pages, you'll find the information you need. If you're unable to find this information, you can request this information from your supplier, and in theory, your request should be provided in a matter of days. If your supplier is unwilling or hesitant to share this information, your safest bet is to find an alternative supplier for that particular service.

Set up your Professional Image and Status

You've done it! If you've made it this far and come through the heavy details of beginning your business, here's a reward for you. This is the step in which you set up aspects of your business that really start to make it take shape and dimension and make it feel real. With your business structure, licence, insurance, and PRS membership out of the way, it's time to bring your business to life. Here are six strides to take that will feel really good.

Business Banking

If you've chosen to operate as a sole trader, setting up a business banking account is advised but not mandatory. On the other hand, if you've chosen to operate as a limited company or a partnership, a business banking account is required. Here again, is a small lesson to learn from my own mistakes.

Operating as a sole trader out of your own personal banking account might feel nice when the money goes in, but the good feeling pretty much ends there. Keeping track of your business finances through your own banking account is a mess and a headache for you, and especially for your accountants and bookkeepers. Operating out of your own personal banking account is also restrictive and perhaps even a violation according to your bank. When you operate a business from a personal bank account, banks aren't too fond. There's probably a stipulation in your bank's terms and conditions which states that your personal banking account is for *personal* use only. Further, a personal banking account won't cut it if you want to apply for business loans or take credit card payments from your clients.

My advice: just get the business banking account. The cost is very minimal and the setup protects you better and often comes with a variety of business banking solutions that will make your life easier and your business grow faster. Your business income and expenses will quickly become a hassle to track, especially if you're managing multiple properties and tenants. This is going to cause serious complications when the time comes to submit accurate tax returns.

Bookkeeping

Okay, maybe not the most enjoyable reward, but it does bring life to your operation to start getting numbers on the books. But how? This relatively complicated process is made super-simple with software. QuickBooks (https://quickbooks.com) is the most popular solution for small businesses. QuickBooks even offers additional features and support for those working in the sublet vertical, so it's basically a perfect place to start. In previous years, QuickBooks was a piece of software that required your purchase and download, but as the cloud has become more versatile and reliable, so too has QuickBooks. It's now available online and without download so that you can access it from any browser and device. An account only takes about 5 minutes to set up and link with your bank.

QuickBooks makes it simple to manage your business' income and expenses, invoices, taxes, reporting and analytics, receipts, 1099s, bills, and projected profitability. Perhaps the best news is that within your account, user permissions can be granted. This is excellent functionality if you want to share access to this account with partners or accountants and bookkeepers, especially if you want to protect sensitive information. QuickBooks can even help you find a bookkeeper to manage this for you if it's in your budget. There are many packages from which to select starting under £20/month for a basic start and ranging to about £100/month for advanced options, such as a complete payroll automation package. The cost of QuickBooks is tax-deductible for your business and free phone, email, and chat support is included in your free trial and purchase.

Even if QuickBooks doesn't sound like the right option for you, there are alternative software applications to select from. My personal advice, however, is that QuickBooks is the most trusted, most widely used, and provides the most functionality for the fairest cost, so it's a no-brainer.

Contact Information

Now that you're official it's time to look official and this is a lot more fun than bookkeeping. Get yourself a business phone number and a business email address. Both are pretty simple to secure, you just need to make a few choices about how you want this to go. Often times, a rent-to-rent business professional just starting out will use a personal cell phone number and email address. There's nothing wrong with this as a sole trader, but if you're operating as a limited company or partnership, you're going to need official contact information anyway. One thing to think about if you're going to start with the email and phone number you already have, is that now the public essentially has access to your personal number and email address and this can soon become rather annoying, especially if you like to keep your personal life separate from your business life.

Another detail to consider if you're using your own email address is professionalism. You don't want to be dispensing an email address that looks unprofessional, overly-revealing, or offensive. This is very easily avoided and free to overcome. Create a free and separate email address for your business communications with Gmail, or any other number of email client services. It used to be thought that an address ending with "@gmail.com" looked unprofessional but that belief has in large part disappeared, and you'll find many professionals now use Gmail and the like for their business email. Email from your business account can even be forwarded to your personal account and filtered appropriately so you don't have to check multiple accounts throughout your day.

A third option, and my personal favourite is that when you acquire a website domain and host, you often get a free email account (or multiple) that matches your site. This is the most professional image. Your email will look something like: John@website.com, where the "website" will be your domain name and will match your site and business name.

Business phone numbers work in much the same way. Your phone provider can often offer you a secondary number at a lower cost and bundle it into your monthly bill. The phone number can be forwarded to your cell or another phone line and you'll be able to easily determine if someone is calling you for personal interaction or business interaction by which number they called, even if it all goes to the same line. It's essentially like using an alias phone number. If you're really lucky, sometimes a website even comes with a phone number, though these offers are more costly and harder to find.

Answering Services

At first, it might sound like an answering service is an unnecessary expense, but as you become busier with work, it will sound like a godsend. The truth is that most of these services are actually very affordable and can be as low as £25/month. If your rent-to-rent business is a side business at this point, an answering service makes even more sense. If prospects and clients call while you're at your other job, someone is still there to answer and direct the call or take the message professionally. Answering services offer a host of features, but you'll want to look for one that offers a reasonable price, a live receptionist (24/7 is even better), tailored care, ease-of-use, and excellent customer support. One of the best I've had the pleasure of using previously was (https://www.takemycalls.co.uk/) which offers an enormous amount of service and features for a very low and reasonable rate. As you grow, these services can scale with you to support your growing needs.

Regardless of the business structure you operate under, an answering service is not a mandatory requirement, but it sure does help your professional image. If TakeMyCalls doesn't look right for you, search for some of their competitors and see if you can find an offer that works perfectly for you as you're starting out. Remember that you can always start with a basic package to try it out and increase features and services as needed. When prospects and clients call for information and help, they may not get the answer they need at that moment, but hearing someone on the other end of the phone, as opposed to a voicemail message, instils a greater deal of confidence in you and your business and it cultivates a feeling of being taken care of at the moment. Many of these services even integrate with other applications like your CRM, so that each call is recorded and listed under the proper contact, so you'll always be able to reference who called, when, and why from your CRM database, and you can track whether the call request has been resolved or still needs your attention.

Online Presence

Though it is not mandatory for any business type, you'll soon find it's pretty difficult to market your business without some form of an online presence. Most often, this is a website, but it can be something a simple as a Facebook or LinkedIn account for your business. A dedicated website certainly looks most professional, but that's not to say you can't sculpt your social media to look highly professional as well. Truly, the key is professionalism.

Creating a professional business site is easy if you know-how and have the time, but if you don't, you can again turn to freelance sites like Fiverr to find a professional that can build this for you. If you need to do this yourself for budgetary reasons, there's still a wealth of tools to help. You'll be responsible for purchasing a domain and finding a host. In most cases, the vendor from which you purchase your domain (such as GoDaddy.com) also offers hosting services. Your website domain can be as little as £5 annually, and hosting services usually cost around £10-20/month. The cost of your domain will largely depend on the keywords you want to use and the suffix you select. Words that are more popular and have a greater demand are going to cost more. A suffix like ".com", as opposed to ".biz" is also going to cost a bit more. This is where it takes a little bit of creativity to come up with a website name that's not already taken, and not unreasonably expensive. The possible combinations are infinite, and with a little focus, you'll find something that fits you perfectly. Avoid creating a domain that's hard to read, type, spell or has numbers or symbols in it. These cause undue hassle in the marketing process. If you don't have a domain, you don't need a host and if you don't get a host, there's no reason to buy a domain. This is one reason vendors offer them together.

Creating an entire website when you don't have all that much to say yet can be a big project. You'll want to incorporate a fair amount of web content and imagery that supports your business, such as images of your properties. Writing the content and adding the pictures can be time-consuming. This is another good reason to seek out a freelancer for help. However, there's another popular option. You can create a web presence for your business with one landing page rather than an entire site. You'll still need to acquire a domain and hosting, but there will be a lot less to set up and manage, and a landing page can still display and capture everything you need to get the job done. Selecting a landing page can be a perfect start to your business and then in the future, once you've grown in experience and size, you can switch to a full site if necessary.

If you choose to create a presence for your business using a social media platform (or several), this cuts the cost significantly. You won't need to acquire a domain or hosting, but keep in mind you won't have as much freedom naming your profile link or suffix. Still, your presence can look mighty professional, and again, if you don't have time to do this setup yourself, a freelancer can help you for a nominal fee. With a social media platform, you also don't need to worry so much about GDPR compliance because when an individual visits a platform like Facebook, LinkedIn, YouTube, or Instagram, consent is implied. However, if you employ or link to business forms from the social media site, you'll still need to make sure to include the proper opt-out options on your forms.

Whichever option you go with, having an online presence in today's world is almost a necessity, especially if you plan to market online. Further, a web presence builds a rapport and sense of ease and trust with your prospects and clients. Pick something that fits your budget to start and bring your business to life online.

Business Cards

Last but not least, get some business cards made up so you can hand them to prospects, clients, and colleagues when networking and conducting business. Providing a business card will make a great impression and make it very easy for your clients and prospects to get in touch with you. Your card should be professional yet eye-catching and memorable. There are plenty of custom card creation tools and printing options available online, but one of the easiest and least expensive options is Vistaprint (https://www.vistaprint.com). This site allows you to customise the look of your card, front and back, and set the number of cards you want to be printed. Better yet, Vistaprint is almost always offering discounts and deals. A pack of 500 cards can often cost you as little as £10-20 depending on the customisation and number of cards.

If actual cards aren't really your preference, the world of technology has you covered with digital business cards. You can design a business card online that can be given digitally to your clients and prospects. There are benefits to this route, as well. Mainly, the card rarely is lost since it's in the cloud. Plus, no printing means your operation is that much eco-friendlier. Still, it can take a little getting used to, for you to give and for others to receive. Transferring your digital business card from your phone to a prospect's phone at a networking event sounds good, but you don't want to be fumbling with your phone, or making them fumble with yours. Sometimes the old way is still the best and handing someone a traditional business card can be the simplest and most professional option.

You're only half-way done, and you've accomplished so much already! At this point, your rent-to-rent business is fully set up and operational — time to get to work.

Chapter 4:
5-Step Process to Find Rental Properties

Your business is registered, insured, and you've joined the redress scheme. Your 12-month business plan is written, and your contracts are gathered. Your sublet model is selected. You have a strong understanding of the rules and regulations you must follow. Your business presence is established. Time to put everything in motion, find some properties in some lucrative locations, and make some money.

In this section, I'll go over the five steps you will take every time you search for new properties to sublet. Over the next year, you will repeat these steps and learn their nuances. This will allow you to refine your process. By refining your process, you will continuously find properties that are more and more attractive, in better and better locations. By polishing these steps, your process becomes sharper, cuts faster, and slices a larger piece of the pie.

Step 1: Location, Location, Location

Even if you've never heard of subletting until now, you know the expression. What are the three most important factors in real estate? Location.

The first step is to find three lucrative areas that are nearby enough for you to reach easily. Go out far enough that you're reaching profitable zones, but not so far that they're inconvenient.

You're looking for locations that offer a higher rental cost. Aim for locations that are already affluent, unless one of your missions is to better communities through property management. Don't get too selective. It's a bit like shopping in the market. You want a high-quality brand, but maybe not the highest quality. For a beginner, aim for a location you would rate 4 or 5 stars; a place you might even like to live.

I'll point out now, it can be a smart idea to search for locations you might rate 3 stars. These places have often got a lot of room for improvement, and your preparation and early expertise will work for you here. These places are also often targets of tenants because the cost is lower, but the location and properties are still something they can work with and see their families in. This gives you the opportunity to work your negotiation skills and strike a bargain with property owners for a lower guaranteed rent, but a professional and well-managed property. When they get a load of your preparedness and expertise, the offer will very likely look appealing to them. Be careful, and make sure your property owners are on the up and up as well as you.

Start with about 10 locations you're pretty sure would offer a handsome profit. Then begin knocking down one after the other until you have the three best locations left. You will filter your 10 locations out by studying a few key factors for each of them. Over time, and depending on your general location, you'll be able to find which factors are really the best for determining prime location. To start off, investigate the following for each location:

- Average annual household income
- Average cost of buying a home
- Average mortgage rates
- Average rental cost
- Tax history
- Average tenant turnover rates
- Rise in home values
- Rise in rental values
- Job availability
- Unemployment rates
- Nearby school systems and ratings
- Nearby universities and ratings
- Public transportation
- Public resources
- Crime rates
- Utilities access and average costs

One by one, decide if the location is good enough for you. Put it on the keep list or in the bin until you're left with your three perfect starting locations.

Step 2: Find Viable Properties

You're looking for properties that will match your budget and bandwidth, but still deliver a handsome monthly profit in any of the three locations you've decided upon.

Find your properties with three basic tactics. Dig through local listings, market your business to these three locations, and network in these areas.

Dig

The internet is an endless resource, but visit these locations and pick up local printed listings as well. Use both as it's often the case that the best properties are listed in one but not the other. Think of how you would find an apartment if you were a tenant, find some that have come available (or will), and then find out who owns them and contact those people with your offer.

Market

Whatever you've decided your marketing plan to be, apply it to these three areas. Consider direct mail marketing to related businesses and property owners and customise the marketing to fit the correct audience. Consider running Google Ads or Facebook Ads for your offer in these three locations. Look for landlord listings online and send them directly or email marketing for your offer. It's a numbers game; the more people exposed to your offer, the more that will take it.

Network

Take time to network online and in real life, in these locations. Online, again, the possibilities never end. Use your business LinkedIn profile and network the hell out of it. LinkedIn is the Facebook of the professional world. The platform is built on the idea of growing your network quickly. You really can't afford to not use it.

Similarly, Facebook is loaded with groups you can join for networking in the industry and related industries, and in the exact locations you're targeting. I repeat, "related industries". Don't stop your network at real estate and property management; think of everyone these individuals interact with on a professional level. A local cleaning service or repairman might be your link to the perfect landlord and the perfect property. Network in real life. Find related networking events in the three locations you're targeting and attend them. Go prepared with your business card and perhaps a one-page piece of marketing to quickly illustrate your amazing offer. This could even be a version of your direct mail marketing.

Step 3: Investigate Relevant Local Codes and Regulations

You already know what you're responsible for in terms of overall legal regulations for your business and operations, but there could be a different game afoot in your chosen locations. Do a bit of homework on the local laws, codes, and regulations as they relate to subletting. If there are other rules to be aware of and adhere to, build these into your 12-month plan when you land a property there.

Step 4: Size Up Local Competition

While you're sizing things up, don't forget the local competition. Who else in these three areas is making an offer like yours? How long have they been operating? What does their online presence look like? Which properties do they maintain? Are there reviews of the competition? Do a mini SWOT analysis, but on them. Get to know them at networking events. Sometimes the competition can become your best friend.

Step 5: Run the Numbers

As prospects begin to line up, get a sense for the financial aspects you're working with and start to run some numbers. Outline what you think a great offer would be for guaranteed rent and the property management service you'll offer to supplement it. Outline what you think a competitive but enticing offer will be for your subletters. Outline a projected income to cost estimate. Consider your payback periods on anything you've used to start your business. Generate for yourself a cheat sheet of these points so that when you actually throw out the bait to your prospect, you have an aim.

That's it. Five steps and you're ready to make an offer to your property owners and subletters. These are the five steps that, over the course of your first year, you will become very familiar with through constant repetition each time you go out for more property. This repetition will cause you to sharpen your skills in these areas and the process will start to go faster and more efficiently. Remember, if you can - delegate. Paying a virtual assistant to gather, organise, and filter any of the information in these steps in a way that will speed up the ultimate decision-making process for you, is worth the cost. Especially with your healthy growing profit.

Chapter 5:
Your Viewing and Signing Process

Now that you've found a few properties in your three initial locations, it's time to check them out and negotiate a deal with the property owners. Once your agreements have been made with your property owners or landlords, it's time to get prospective tenants through the doors to view each unit and find the perfect match between landlord - you - tenant - and the unit and location itself. In this section, we'll take a look at the steps you will take to negotiate with your landlords and property owners. Then, I'll walk you through the details of viewing your units with prospective tenants, screening those tenants, and signing a rental agreement with them. With these steps done, you're ready to start collecting rent and managing your properties.

Viewing and Negotiations with Property Owners

Let's assume you've contacted a handful of property owners with your initial offer of managing their property and tenancies and they've taken the bait. You've been in communication with the property owners and it's time for you to view the properties and strike a deal. Now I'll walk you through exactly what you should be thinking and doing to make sure this interaction goes smoothly and professionally with each of your property owners.

Prepare for the Interaction

First things first. Preparation. Nothing can make a prospective property owner more sceptical of your offer than making it up on the spot. Of course there are almost always unforeseen changes and considerations that will affect your final offer and contract, but if you don't walk in with some sort of benchmark on what you're looking to do in profit and management in general, you'll almost certainly end up with a heap of management work and expenses but a rental that will leave you still struggling for profit. Set yourself for success before you meet with the property owner by bringing with you the numbers you've started to run on other units in the area - and don't just bring them - keep the key points in mind as you view the property and discuss possibilities with your prospective owner. Your key points are going to be:

- How long is the term of rental for you?
- What needs to be done to the property to rent it out?
- What is the cost of guaranteed rent you're expecting?
- Does the owner own outright, or are they mortgaging the property?
- Is the property properly insured?
- What has been the average cost to rent this unit in the past for tenants?
- Is there additional management, utilities, security issues you need to act on?

The idea is to get a good sense of what it will take to rent the property, what level of work will be involved to make the unit ready and then manage it going forward, and of course, what kind of profit will you be making after these management costs have been covered.

It's also a smart idea to bring a copy of your business plan, for your reference, but perhaps also for the prospective owner to skim through if they should have in-depth questions. Typically, they will not have in-depth questions at this point. When you hand them your contractual offer for signing, that's when the questions will come, but it's always better to be prepared; not to mention it conveys a much more professional and experienced image to come with these details in hand. At this point, your prospective owners want to know that your operation is legitimate and that you're not going to cause them a loss or undue stress and management themselves. They may want to know why your offer is better than hiring an agency to rent out the property. You know the answer to this is your sweet-as-honey deal which includes guaranteed rent, zero-gap loss, and responsible management. These are not offers a typical agency will make. The agency helps to fill the unit with properly screened tenants, and that's about where the agency offer ends.

Your figures are prepared and in mind; what else needs your preparation before you meet with the prospective property owner? Yourself. Don't show up in street clothes. It seems like it goes without saying, but it happens often and kills the deal before it began. This is the time when your personal appearance will work for you or against you, so dress appropriately and communicate deliberately, both in terms of body language and verbal language. Your appearance should be professional but approachable. You don't necessarily need to throw on the executive 3-piece suit, but if you'd wear it to the gym or lounging around your home, it's out. Go with clean, crisp, business casual. Are you arriving by car? Consider cleaning out your vehicle and sending it through a wash before you show up. These are the small and significant details that help others to form an opinion about you, so don't neglect them.

Viewing the Property

In some cases, you may be viewing a property that is currently occupied by a tenant. Be respectful. Find out if any current tenants will be continuing their rentals, or if they will be leaving soon.

While viewing the property with the property owner, you'll want to view every single space in the unit that you'll be responsible for managing. This includes the sometimes overlooked utilities closest, the attic, the basement, security systems, and the yard and the perimeter of the property. Get an idea of how and when waste and rubbish are removed and the cost of doing so. Find out if the previous tenants have had pets and children if possible. This can also help you gauge any repairs or fixes that might be needed before showing the property to prospective tenants. Does the owner currently (or have they in the past) hire landscapers to take care of the outside of the property, will this responsibility now fall upon you and your property management, and what's the general expense of this upkeep?

Inside the unit, be sure to check every room and pay additional attention to the kitchen and bathroom, as these are almost always where you find expensive repairs that may be needed before you're able to rent the unit again. While assessing needed repairs, consider larger alterations that might be necessary to turn a traditional AST property into an HMO, for example. Note windows, doors, and locks. Will any need replacing to make the property safe and secure again? Door locks almost always need replacing for the safety and security of your next tenants. Ask your property manager to show you how heating, gas, and electric works for the unit, and get a feel for whether you'll be taking on these utilities or if the owner plans to keep them in his or her own name. Typically, the owner can't wait to get rid of extra bills, so it sweetens the deal for them if you're willing to transfer the utilities to yourself or the next tenant.

As you go through the property, you'll be keeping in mind expenses as you go, but take notes. The mind will inevitably forget or mix up details, especially if you're viewing multiple properties with multiple managers. Write your notes down as you're viewing. When you get back to the office to draw up an official contract, these notes are invaluable. One detail you forgot to note can set your whole plan akimbo and skew the profit you were set on.

Assess Your Timeframe

The length of time in which you have to work, to fill the unit, is key. You'll need to consider when current tenants will be out if the unit is occupied. You'll need to determine how long you have once they are gone to make repairs and alterations if any are necessary. Map out how long those fixes will take and what you'll be responsible for paying for during that time. Once those changes are made, you'll need time to show and sign the unit. Consider all of these aspects on your timeframe so you know roughly when you're looking to start making a profit. The bottom line is: how long until you can collect your first payment from your new tenant?

Questions and Insights

Don't be fearful of asking questions. A legitimate owner is going to be happy to share whatever information they can to get a trustworthy manager and a guaranteed rent. The more relevant questions you ask about the history of the unit, the better it is for both of you. Not only does this demonstrate what a conscientious professional you are, but often details will come from these questions that can help you to bargain for a better contract with them. For example, if you need to perform repairs that will equal a significant amount, you may be able to bargain for a lower guaranteed rent in your first year, and this leaves room for the owner to raise it reasonably for you in the second year.

As long as you keep the questions reasonable (don't get overly personal), you really can't ask too many questions. As you move through the property and talk with the owner, questions will come to you. Ask them as they come and take notes. At the start of this process, you may be nervous about whether you're asking the right questions. Remember that you're prepared and educated on the topic; you're asking the right questions if it's giving you insight. As you practice this process over the next year, you'll get the hang of what to ask and what you can leave out. Keep in mind that sometimes the significance of a question can change from location to location, from unit to unit, and from sublet model to sublet model.

The Contract and the Close

In some cases, though typically rarer, you may be able to go for the close on the spot. However, this means you've come with a contract for each of you to sign, and you're confident the owner wants to make a decision today. In a case such as this, more than likely, you've done the majority of your question-asking and profit-and-expense-figuring before you even get to the unit. You've already drawn up the contract for signing.

However, it's a tricky job to write up a final contract without knowing the deal with the property so my advice, at least to start, is: don't count on signing today. Instead, gather every last shred of information you need and then inform the owner you'll be sending a contract for consideration and signing within the next 24 hours.

Back at the office, take the time to consider all of your notes, all of the other properties you're aiming for or already managing, your timeframe, and your expenses. With time to consider these and plot out your expected income and costs, you can confidently draw up a contract that will suit you and the owner, and make the deal a no-brainer for them. Send the offer via email within the 24-hour period you indicated, and then allow your owner another 24 hours to review this offer. It may seem like a fast process, but you also don't want to give your owner enough time to reconsider or drag their heels. After the 24 hours you've allocated for the owner to review the offer, call them. This is your closing call.

A word of warning here: no matter how enthusiastic your in-person meeting is, you cannot count on this alone. Often, property owners (or people in general) want to naturally convey a friendly and positive attitude in such an interaction. Individuals tend to avoid confrontation, so a sunny disposition upfront doesn't always mean your owner carries that through the next 48 hours. Expect that when the owner is alone with time to review the offer, that questions and concerns of their own will pop up and you need to be at the ready to stanch them. If the enthusiasm has dwindled, the closing call is your chance to rejuvenate it.

As you go into your call, your number one goal is this: do not sell your offer. Sell their solution. The property owner is interested in your offer because it solves a number of their own problems. Use this call to remind them (directly and indirectly) of these problems and your solutions for them. Focus on them, not you, and not your deal. You're always pitching the solution to these problems, not your contract. When concerns and objections arise, do not try to skip over them; address them. Suggest a way that these concerns would be alleviated through your management. Illustrate how these concerns are covered in your solutions. If you sense hesitation, ask the prospect to share their thoughts with you. "Tell me your thoughts" is a powerful phrase to demonstrate caring, but more so for you to read your prospect and what's holding them back from signing.

As you speak with your prospective owner on your closing call, do more listening than talking. Much will be revealed to you about any apprehensions at this moment. Don't get trigger-happy; don't get trigger-shy. Utilise the following closing tactics with calm and steady determination, and you'll hit the mark.

Yes or No

Avoid asking questions that result in a yes/no answer. This is a trick I learned going way back to cold-calling and appointment-setting days. Here's an example: "Do you want to meet with our rep to find out how he can save you money?" That's going to be a "yes" or a "no", and guess which one it probably is. After a hefty number of "no"s, I learned to adjust my phrasing. "Do you want to meet with our rep Tuesday or Friday?" Now you've given the prospect a choice, but both choices will equal a "yes". The hefty collection of "no" soon became a hefty collection of "yes". Don't feel bad about it, either. It's often the case that the prospect does actually want your help, but they've been preconditioned to suss out scams and protect themselves. It's going to take your clever phrasing and communication to break through those protective barriers discreetly, to truly help them.

Problem Solver

Reiterate, directly or subtly, the problems and challenges you know your prospect faces, and how your offer solves these. If the problem that causes hesitation is X, demonstrate how your offer covers X with a solution, or how you can work that into the plan. Eliminate X in their mind. To draw out these concerns and set them clear as solved in the prospect's mind, try getting them to say your solution. Try to draw this out with phrases like:

- "Is there any reason why not?"
- "If you were to do this, how will it help you?"
- "If I can find a way to address X, would you sign the agreement by [tomorrow]?"
- "In your opinion, does this solve all of your problems?"

Use Help

"Help" is a magic word. Whether you're offering it or asking for it, the word "help" can take the individual from off the defensive and protective track of mind, and reposition them to a more humanistic and empathetic track of mind. "Would you like my help?" is a fantastic question, because whether they say it or not, they do want help. They are waiting for someone to come along and solve their problems. The idea that a problem-solver is right in front of them (literally or figuratively) is very tempting. The prospect considers how wonderful it would feel to get the thing they want: a problem solver. They do want your help or you would not have made it this far with this prospect.

"Can I help you?" is great, but you know what's even more powerful? "I need your help." Convey that the plan you've laid out is all the help they need, but you need a bit of help from them. Accentuate that you need a small piece of help from them to get this wonderful plan underway, and that help is to approve the agreement with their signature.

Here Today, Gone Tomorrow

One of your best friends in negotiations and closing is the scarce deal. Introduce scarcity to help nudge your prospect along. Whether you're selling widgets or a 5-star property management package, knowing that the deal is fleeting will set fire under your prospect. Here's the opportunity, don't let it pass you by. There are several ways to convey this, but here are a few key phrases to try out:

- "This opportunity is going to help some property owner in [location], I don't see why it shouldn't be you"
- "I'd hate to see you stay stuck where you are...let's take the step now to prevent that."
- "I know you want a solution in place by [date] so with that in mind, perhaps we should move to the final agreement and get the ball rolling."

If, Then

The If/Then setup is often used to drive the point home toward the end of the conversation. It's a tool to remind the prospect again, if you continue down the same path, then you get the same results. That's assuming the results have been less than desirable, like a vacant unit. You can set the phrasing up to be something like: "If you pass on this deal, then you can expect more of what you've had; a vacant unit; an unmanaged unit; rent without guarantee". Don't be too harsh, but don't be afraid of being direct.

Let It Go

If you've pulled out all the stops and you still get hesitation and delay, don't obsess on it; move on. It's not the right deal for you, and that delay could be a sign of worse struggles to come with that property owner. It's not worth your precious time. You know your offer is excellent so take it to someone else who recognises its worth.

Viewing and Negotiations with Tenants

Let's assume you've signed with your property owner and it's time to start showing your unit to prospective tenants. There are two major ways this can go: showing a unit while it's still occupied, or when it's vacant. Showing a unit when it's vacant is a much more desirable scenario, but we work with what we have.

There are benefits to both, though my personal opinion is that despite its minor disadvantages, showing a vacant space is better. If the accommodation is still occupied when you show it, at least the likelihood of a tenancy gap and rent loss is lessened. Another minor benefit is that your utility transfer will only be from the last tenant to the next, and you'll not need to be the middleman on that. This is, however, null if you plan to keep the utilities in your name and add that into the cost of the unit for the next tenant. On the other hand, if you have to show the accommodation when there's a tenant still occupying it, there's no real guarantee it will be clean and presentable. Further, the tenant may not be co-operative and could try to sabotage the viewing. Worse still, the tenant may be late in leaving, which will compromise the date your new tenant is supposed to move in. One tactic I've found that works well in these scenarios is a friendly little incentive. Consider how far it can go when you offer a gift card to the current tenant, for a nice restaurant or a local shop to furnish the new space that the old tenant will be moving to. A £25-50 gift card can make your transition smooth and easy. Keep in mind though that another drawback that comes with an immediate transfer from old tenant to new is the lack of time in between tenancies where you're able to get in there to clean and make repairs and changes. This, specifically, will be an aspect of the sublet you need to keep in mind and work out with your new tenant.

If you are working with a tenant that currently occupies the space, be respectful to their space. Communicate clearly and well ahead of time when you plan to show the unit. Ask the current tenant to pick up the accommodation and secure any animals that might be in the unit. If there's a tenant occupying the space, it's a bad idea to post "For Rent" signs outside the apartment. This inevitably leads to random individuals walking up to the unit as asking the current tenant about renting and viewing the apartment. Not only is this a hassle for the current tenant, but it spoils your hard work. You don't know what that tenant will say to your prospect or if they'll even be friendly.

Don't leave this to chance. Place your ads in print and online and direct interested parties to contact you directly via phone or email. This way, a viewing time can be set that works for all parties involved.

If the unit is vacant, you risk losing money on rent and you'll likely have to pay for the utilities to stay on between tenancies, but the benefits are worth it, in my opinion. Vacant accommodation gives you the opportunity to get in there and make appropriate repairs and to clean the accommodation. This can often include minor fixes and painting, rug cleaning, tile replacement, cabinet door replacement, and so forth. This can be quite a bit harder to manage if your new tenant has already moved in.

With a vacant space, you have the opportunity to not only clean, but stage the accommodation so that it's warm, cosy, and inviting. The right staging can help prospective tenants to imagine themselves in the unit living happily with furnishings and accoutrements they want to live with and enjoy. Not only can you control the look and feel of the accommodation, but you can control how the accommodation smells and how warm and inviting it is when prospective tenants enter. Another benefit to working with vacant accommodation is that scheduling is quite a bit easier. This may translate to a gap in the tenancy for a brief time, but trying to schedule a time to show the unit that works for all parties can end up causing significant delay.

Now let's assume that whether the accommodation is vacant or not, you have prospective tenants lined up to see it. What do you need to do?

Legally, you need to show each and every space/room that the tenant will have access to, including storage, basement, attic, garden, everything. If they can go into the space in their tenancy, you need to show that space during the viewing.

What's more, steering a prospect is bad form and it can just as easily set you up for liability. Steering is trying to show off a certain part of the accommodation whilst skipping over other parts that are perhaps not as attractive or convenient. However, doing this can actually be construed as discrimination. For example, if a prospective tenant comes to see the accommodation and that individual is disabled in some way, and you avoid showing the individual a part of the unit, it could be seen as a liability for which you can suffer consequences before you've even begun to rent. Avoid this by showing every prospective tenant every inch of space they will have access to.

Prepare for Questions from the Tenant

Do you remember the list of important aspects you used to find your location and the property? Your prospective tenants will have the same concerns so you should have as much of that information at the ready as possible. Anticipate the questions your tenants will bring to you, and beat them to the punch. If you can, demonstrate the answer during the showing. If the question happens to be about a security gate, show the prospective tenant what they need to know about the security for the accommodation. If you cannot demonstrate, have facts handy. A tenant may ask you about local school systems or public transportation. Prepare by gathering these details before you meet so that your prospective tenant gets the information they need, and you look like a professional.

Know the Area

It's not just the property that tenants want to know about. Especially if they're moving a significant distance from their last residence, prospective tenants want to know about the great location you're working in and what it has to offer. Prepare your notes or do a little internet research before you meet with tenants and prepare for questions like:

- What are the schools like in the area?
- Is there public transportation?
- Are there any local parks?
- Are there any local gyms?
- What's the crime rate like? Burglaries?
- Are there any noise nuisances? High traffic? Nightclubs?
- Is the area prone to flooding and other natural disasters?
- What are the neighbours like?

Exterior Property

The exterior of the property is the first thing prospects will see so if you can, clean up and repair this area as well and stage it. It doesn't have to be much. Depending on the exterior, you may need to make fence or gate repairs, mailbox repairs, garden and lawn maintenance and anything else that draws the eye in a negative way. Better yet- anything with the potential to draw the eye in a positive way should be the things you focus on. Showing the exterior will give you an opportunity to answer questions like:

- Who is responsible for garden maintenance?
- Is there an extra cost for it?
- Is it shared?
- Are tenants allowed to garden?

- Should tenants expect any upcoming exterior repairs or changes?
- How is the exterior of the unit secured? Gates? Door and window locks? Security and alarm systems? Floodlights?
- Has the unit ever had a break-in?

Interior Property

The inside of the property is where tenants typically have the most questions and concerns. If you've had the opportunity to repair and clean the unit and stage it, you could very well head off these questions simply by appearances. Still, be ready to address some of the more pressing concerns that typically come up. Prepare to answer questions like:

- Are there any signs of dampness or mould?
- Are any repairs still required?
- Are tenants allowed to paint the walls?
- Does the unit come furnished in any way? Does it come with basic appliances?
- Is there central heating? Do the radiators all work? Where are they throughout the home?
- How's the water pressure and hot water? Are there any leaky pipes or dripping taps? Do sinks and showers drain well?
- Is the accommodation insulated? Are there any draughts?
- Is there storage space? Is it shared?
- Can tenants put up shelving, decor, and curtains?

Security, Safety, and Utilities

When you take over accommodation, the safety and security regulations are a very significant responsibility for you. All relevant regulations must be met and sometimes this means replacing old fire alarms and making sure fire exits are easily accessible. If the accommodation is to be rented as an HMO, there are some additional security and safety issues you may need to address. For example, fire alarms, extinguishers, and blankets must be available in the accommodation for emergencies. Take time to go through these aspects of the property as you show it to prospective tenants. Be prepared to answer questions like:

- Does the accommodation include fire alarms? How many? Have they been tested?
- Are there fire extinguishers in the accommodation? How many?
- Are there fire blankets in the kitchen and elsewhere?
- Are fire regulations adhered to and addressed?
- Are there carbon monoxide detectors in the accommodation?
- Where are the fire exits and how accessible are they?
- Have you got a current Landlords gas certificate?
- Have you undertaken a Legionnaires' disease risk assessment?
- Are there any electrical wiring or outlet concerns? How many outlets are there throughout the unit?
- Are there working telephone and cable points in the unit?
- How's the Wi-Fi signal?
- How does waste removal work?

The Agreement and the Costs

The prospective tenant will undoubtedly have questions of their own, but this is a good opportunity for you to ask questions of the tenant. Questions will go both ways and this is a great way for you to pre-screen tenants for whether or not they'll be a good match for the unit and your management. Focus on setting proper expectations up front to gauge how well your prospect accepts them. Share and collect information on the following points:

- How much is the rent each month?
- Is a first, last, and secure payment required? How much are they?
- Are pets allowed? Is there an additional cost for pets?
- Are utilities included in the cost or are they separate? Is the tenant responsible for them? What are the average utility costs for the unit?
- Are there additional costs to the accommodation the tenant is responsible for?
- Is there a late fee for rent paid late?
- Is there a tenancy agreement that can be shared for review?

Finding Tenants and Conducting Viewings

You now have a solid understanding of many of the questions and aspects that will come up as you show the accommodation to prospective tenants, but let's take a moment to go over a well-organised and deliberate showing. First of all, you need to find some potential tenants. Obviously using agents to list a property or bedroom incurs a fee, which will eat into your profits. If listing the whole property, you can use Facebook Marketplace, Facebook groups in the local area or Gumtree to advertise. If you are using the HMO model, I advise you to do all of the above, in addition to listing each room on www.spareroom.com and other similar websites. These websites are responsible for filling 90% of my vacant rooms, and the turnaround time is incredible. So many young professionals or students are looking for an affordable room because renting a one-bedroom property could cost them three times the amount. For every accommodation you show to someone, you should have a basic plan for how you intend to walk the visitor through the property and all of the areas to which the tenant will have access. You should have an idea of which rooms and features are the most attractive and how you'll highlight them in the viewing process. For example, if one of the nicest areas of the accommodation is perhaps a balcony or a patio, show this space last and invite the tenant to sit and enjoy the space whilst you discuss cost and expectations. Each room in the accommodation will have its key selling features, so include in your viewing plan a way for you to highlight these as well. Traditionally, big selling points include features like:

- Large and open rooms
- Open-floor concepts
- Updated appliances and safety features
- Beautiful views
- Natural lighting
- Rooftop access, courtyards, gardens
- Walk-in wardrobes
- Ample and secured storage areas
- Central heating

Pre-Screening Questions to Ask Prospective Tenants

While you're showing the space, you can and should ask your own set of questions that will gain your insight into the prospect and help you pre-screen them. Start with some general questions that are not so invasive, such as:

- Where are you from?
- Do you come from a large family?
- What do you do for fun?
- What do you do for work?

Then you can start to ease into the more revealing and insightful questions as they pertain to subletting.

- Why are you moving?
- When do you plan to move?
- Are you living in a similar situation now?
- What's the earliest you can move in?
- What's your average monthly income? (The monthly income should be at least double the rent, roughly.)
- Will anyone be moving with you?
- Do you have pets?
- Do you smoke?
- Will you consent to a credit and background check?
- Will you be able to provide references?

From tenant to tenant, be sure to ask the same questions to all. This keeps everything fair and cannot be misconstrued as discrimination. There are other tricks to pre-screening as well, and though they don't involve asking questions, they can be very revealing. Keep a lookout for the following:

The applicant's opinion of the property - If the prospective tenant is overly enthusiastic, it can be a sign that they are lying about their impressions or that they are trying to overcompensate because they know they may have a tarnished rental background. If the individual is overly critical of the property, it may be a sign of a troublesome tenant or an attempt to negotiate a much lower cost of rent.

The applicant's general behaviour - Take note of whether the individual is polite to you and any current tenants that may be present. Similarly, note whether the applicant is respectful of the property; wiping their feet upon entry, closing doors quietly, or whether they make unusual requests. This again can be a sign of a troublesome tenant.

The applicant's appearance and vehicle - If a prospective tenant shows up to a viewing in dirty and dishevelled clothing, and their vehicle looks much the same, this can be a sign that the individual does not take care of themselves and their own property. This is an insight that they may not take care of your property either.

The applicant's preparedness and attentiveness - If a prospective tenant shows up to a viewing unprepared and has no questions, it leaves a lot of room for misunderstandings to grow. An interested tenant will come prepared and will ask relevant questions.

As the viewing process winds down with your prospective tenant, be clear about the next steps. It is at this point that you should communicate whether there is an application fee and ask them to submit an application.

Let the prospective tenant know that as part of the application process, you will be conducting a credit and background check and contacting references. Tenants can negotiate costs and other terms of your agreement, but do not feel as though you have to bend to these. It's much cleaner to require the same from every tenant that applies for the space. It's more than okay to explain to the prospect that these are the steps your business has put in place for the benefit and safety of all parties involved. Further, you can explain that by following these steps you're ensuring that each applicant is treated fairly and equally, and this is a requirement of the law. Allowing one applicant to skip the background check, for example, can be seen as a sign of discrimination, for which your business can be fined and penalised.

As a professional subletter, remember to not make any tenancy decisions on the spot, especially without having conducted the background check. Instead, let the applicant know you'll be conducting the checks over the course of the next day or so and that you'll be back in touch to let them know how it goes and whether you'd like to proceed with them. A phone call or email will be appropriate. Let applicants know how to contact you should more questions arise over the next few days.

Chapter 6:
Scaling for Success

You've made it to the last step in your successful path to profitable subletting and property management; preparing for greatness and growth in the coming business quarters and years to come. Though it may be a bit early for you to take action on any of these aspects of your business just yet, you should have them in mind and build them into your process. So take out that 12-month business plan and let's see where you can add in these ideas and goals.

Expanding Your Property Structure

Up until this point, you've likely been focused on the subletting model because of its ability to make you a fast profit and get your business officially in the door to the industry. As you begin to make a healthy profit and your costs have largely been repaid or dissolved, it's time to think about expanding that which you do. With the profit you make, surely a portion will be put back into the business and this includes more properties. At this point as yourself whether a buy-to-rent unit is within your reach and how it can fit into your plan. With a year of experience behind you, you've developed a solid understanding of what it takes to rent and manage tenants. Now how about making a greater profit in leasing out a unit you've purchased? You essentially become the property owner of a new unit and with all your expertise, can skip the middleman and rent directly to tenants.

A move like this can be risky so it will require a healthy dose of due diligence. If you purchase a place and mortgage it, are you still able to make a healthy profit after expenses? Owning your own property to rent out gives you the benefit of capital growth. The unit will, in theory, grow in value in the coming years and this means a growth in profit via renting or even selling in the future.

Similarly, many who start out with rent-to-rent schemes transition into other real estate ventures such as fix-and-flip properties. In this scenario, you would purchase a property that falls well below the average cost of a new home. These are often properties that have been repossessed for non-payment or failure to adhere to the terms and conditions of a mortgage lender. In these cases, the property will need fixing. Perhaps this will be some interior remodelling or a new roof. Whatever needs to be done, the idea is to get in and do it quickly so that you can reposition the home back on the market. A fix-and-flip investment will obviously cost a fair chunk of money up front to make the repairs, but the profit made selling a home can well exceed what you're making through subletting.

That's not to say you cannot stick with the sublet models and be just as successful. If you've started with an AST sublet, consider adding an HMO or an accommodation model to your portfolio. If you've had success with one sublet model and you want to stick with it, that works, too. Consider your expansion in terms of acquiring more properties to manage. There's really not a wrong way to grow and expand, except for not growing and expanding. Pulling in profit is great, but your business needs direction, and it is through this direction and strategy that even greater profits await you.

Acquire a Team

Another way to grow and expand is to consider adding employees to your payroll. If this is part of your plan, remember that your business structure must be such that you are no longer a sole trader, but making this small business structure change can mean more money faster. When you have a team that you can delegate to, the process goes much faster and you can acquire more properties and tenants at a greater rate. For all the work you'll do yourself over the course of a year, imagine if you could pass the more time-consuming tasks to others. Imagine if you could pay someone else to run your marketing, conduct your viewings, run background checks, and draw up the paperwork? This will leave you open for the heavier business decisions, and the development of your business' next steps. Like the expansion into buy-to-rent or fix-and-flip properties, hiring a team, even a small one, is another upfront business cost you'll incur.

There are business structure costs to handle, such as registering your business, ensuring it for employees, offering at least minimum wage (but probably more for the type of work being done), and offering benefits. If this doesn't seem like a realistic step for your next 12-month business plan, you can start small. Consider continuing your business structure as it is, but hiring a virtual assistant or a freelance assistant to help you with some of your work. This individual can be paid a lower wage while still taking a good deal of time-consuming research and paperwork off of your own plate.

Grow the Marketing Game

At this point, there is perhaps no easier and quicker way to expand than to up your marketing game and keep it fresh. Even if this is the only strategy you act on in your next step to expansion, it is arguably the most important one. In your first year of business, you've been heavy with all of the responsibilities that come with a start-up. Now that these responsibilities have been achieved, you'll find yourself with more bandwidth in year two. Use this time to gain growth through marketing.

Get Intimate with Your Audience

After the time you've spent in the last year getting to know your audience, you've come away with better insights. For your property owners and for your tenants, it's time to refine. You can do this by analysing the top 20% of your customers. Profile them. Who is it that makes up the top 20% of your property owners, and likewise your tenants? Find the similarities amongst these audience members; location, financial aspects, humanistic qualities, wants and goals. By analysing, you'll be able to better pinpoint what makes up your best audience and what makes up the other 80%. It's now your goal to target the individuals that make up that top 20%. Advertise in places they will see. Offer value they seek. Set higher costs that they can still afford. By doing so, you'll be attracting more of the people you want to work with, and less of the people you don't.

Utilise Local Directories

With just a bit of research, you can identify dozens of local directories in which to list your business. Don't limit this to only print; online local directories are just as, if not more, important. But don't neglect print directories, either. Take a look around the communities in which you work and pick up print directories where you can. Listing in these directories is free or possible with a nominal annual fee. Consider listing on directories like:

- Google My Business
- LandlordZone
- CitizensAdvice
- Bing Places
- 118Information
- ThePhoneBook
- Yelp
- FreeIndex
- MyLocalServices
- TouchLocal
- Scoot
- Yell.com
- HotFrog
- Brownbook

Gather Testimonials

You've had ample time to build a rapport with numerous property owners and tenants. Now, ask them for a testimonial. If you want to sweeten the deal, perhaps offer a small monetary compensation, such as a portion discount on rent for the month, or a gift certificate for a local dinner or movie. Ask these individuals to provide a written testimonial to either be given to you for use as you see fit, or online in any of the relevant directories that offer ratings and endorsements. If you have a business website or a social media page, add these testimonials for better exposure to a focused audience.

Website Improvements

Take the time to tune up your website, landing page, or social media accounts. Keep them fresh and relevant and refine the locations you target. Business websites often have opt-in marketing that allows visitors of the site to sign up for newsletters, blogs, and valuable downloadable content. Consider adding or improving these opt-in options and repositioning them on the page for greater visibility and engagement. Sidebars, headers, footers, and banners at the top or bottom of a specific piece of content can work very well. Give them a chance where they are (90 days for example) and then experiment with relocating them. If it's possible, hire a freelance digital marketing pro for their expertise in this area. Often, not only will you gain their expertise, but they often will carry out these steps for you, included in their cost.

Add a Call-to-Action

In addition to opt-in options, a business website, landing page, or social media page often includes at least one call-to-action (CTA). A call to action is an enticing offer that pulls interested parties into your sales circle. For example, you might offer an online tenant application that reduces or eliminates the application fee. This offer can pull in prospective tenants so you have less work to do in the hunt for them.

Radio Advertisement

Radio is not dead. In fact, running your ad or securing a small slot of time to talk with local radio jockeys, on-air can greatly increase your exposure. Despite assumptions, radio advertisements such as this can be more cost-effective than print ads, and it will reach a wider audience. This may not target your refined 20%, but you never know who's listening; a friend or contact of the top 20% could be listening and will happily pass along your information and your offer.

SEO and PPC Strategies

SEO, or Search Engine Optimisation can move you upwards on Google when individuals, both landlords and tenants, search for the services you offer. SEO practices increase the amount of traffic to your site and the quality of those visitors, simply by implementing keywords. The content you display on your site can be optimised to include the words that your audience is searching for so that when these individuals turn to Google for search help, they organically find your site. PPC, or pay-per-click is much like SEO, but monetised. Utilising keywords, advertisers can basically pay for visitors to click on their ads based on the keywords for which the visitor has searched. The ad then directs the visitor to the advertiser's website or landing page for more information, and ultimately, to follow the call to action.

Social Media Marketing Strategy

More and more often, we see local ads placed on Facebook and similar social media platforms. These ads work much the same way as a PPC campaign, but in a location (social media) that your audience is already using. These campaigns are easy to set for your top 20% audience target, as well. Facebook makes it relatively easy to set up these campaigns yourself, and you can run them for as little as £10 per day. Campaigns are generally set for as little as 30 days and during that time, Facebook presents your ad in the feeds of the audience for which you've set your targets. Again, you can do this yourself, or consider hiring a freelance social media manager to set this for you.

Get Involved the Community

When you position yourself in the communities in which you work, not only are you demonstrating your desire and ability to help the local communities, but you're cultivating free (or nearly free) advertisement for your business. Community involvement is an excellent method for building rapport.

Establish Yourself as an Authority
Take time to write a blog or a feature article in a local print. This opportunity can easily establish you as an experienced professional and authority in the industry. If you don't have the time to keep up with a blog, and you don't have the opportunity to write a feature article, consider hosting an online AMA (ask me anything) and inviting interested members of your target audience to participate. Visit sites like Business.com and Quora to find questions that pertain to your industry and answer these questions concisely and professionally. There are plenty of places to assert your authority and professionalism if you just look for them.

Volunteer or Sponsor
Search the communities you currently target or want to target and find local events that your business can volunteer to be a

part of. These events don't need to necessarily be related to your business or industry, in fact, it can work better for you if they are not. If your business is not able to physically participate, sponsor someone locally who can. This can be as easy as agreeing to sponsor someone for a local 5k, craft fair, or cook-off that ultimately benefits the community. By doing this, you expose yourself to a greater portion of the community, and though this may not be your target market, much like the radio, your involvement will get your business noticed and your contact passed along to those in the community that are your target audience.

Contests and Promotions

Beyond getting involved in local events, you can create contests and promotions yourself. It makes sense if these are more directly related to your business. For example, if you're able to build rapport with a local cleaning service or furniture store, you may be able to strike a deal with them to promote their business alongside your own to offer a free cleaning service or furnishings to individuals moving to the area. Combine this with your radio advertising and you've got a successful, simple marketing strategy that's sure to reach a large number of people interested in the contest or promotion.

Advance Yourself

Do not get stagnant and stop learning. There are always new practices, new techniques, and updated regulations in the world of rent-to-rent. There will always be new and changing information you must keep up with in order to stay fresh and relevant and to position yourself and the professional and authority you want to be in your local area(s). You've already learned so much, but it's nothing compared to what you have yet to learn from other professionals, who much like I, can train you to avoid mistakes and capitalise on opportunities.

Training Courses

When the time comes to develop your acumen even further than you have already with the contents of this book, you will find an abundance of resources from which to learn. Online, you can find several courses or webinars pertinent to your study of rent-to-rent and related business. You should, by all means, research the hosts and lecturers of these courses to make sure you're learning from the best, instead of passing your hard-earned profit to a fly-by-night individual trying to make quick cash. Research the course material before you pay for it, to make sure you're not just rehashing information you've already learned and practiced. Find out what the expectations are for you by the end of the course and if it involves any sort of certification or significant accomplishment by the end of the course. Many courses can be taken online, and many of those can be taken at your own pace. One small issue to watch out for in that case, is that sometimes when there is no time limit or accountability, it can be tempting to start the course but never finish it. If this sounds like something you might be guilty of, select a course that requires attendance at a certain time (usually via a webinar or live video call) and your completion of the course materials by a certain deadline.

In addition to online courses, live courses in your local area are often available multiple times a year. These are typically seminars that last one day or several days and by the completion of the course, you're guaranteed some form of certification and supplemental benefits. Not only will an option like this educate you, but it also provides an exclusive networking circle of other local professionals with whom to build a rapport. Courses and seminars that are live and in person can sometimes require the course director to present a higher level of authority and expertise, so though the course may cost a bit more than that of an online course, you may receive a much higher quality of valuable and useful information.

Coaches and Mentors

Courses are great, but the material is designed to meet the needs of everyone. Courses don't do such a good job at analysing your specific circumstances and designed solutions that you specifically need. To get help on a more personal level, seek out a coach or mentor that will work with you directly, on your own 12-month business plan, for a longer period of time; sometimes throughout the entire year and beyond. Indeed, a coach or mentor will likely only support you for a fee, but this is well worth the cost to be able to have an experienced and dedicated professional in your corner.

Your coach or mentor will help you to develop business strategies that will fit your exact goals and budget. This individual will meet with you regularly to build your identity, sharpen your marketing approach, spot strengths, weaknesses, and dangerous gaps in your process. These professionals provide accountability for your progress on these action plans. With your own coach or mentor, you'll build confidence more quickly, and receive the encouragement and tough love needed to succeed.

Property Investment Secrets – Rent to Rent: You've Got Questions, I've Got Answers!

If you've enjoyed this book and you've learned as much from me as I hope you have, one of the best professional advancements you can make is to continue this course of education. The insight and tools I've offered you here do not stop here. You've made it through a wealth of information to begin your business, but now you can take it to the next level in the next book that supplements this one.

In the next book, you'll take what you've learned and distil it. You'll dive deeper into building your next business plan, your next marketing strategy, and your polished online and professional image. As you've read through this book, you've likely come up with some additional questions for each scenario. For example, what does it take to delegate work to a virtual assistant? What kind of work can you delegate? What kind of work is too specific to delegate? You might wonder how to go about devising a sales funnel opportunity on your own business website, and how to build a social media campaign that works effectively and quickly. You might be eager to find out more about what kinds of safety and security codes you'll need to adhere to in order to run the tightest ship possible.

The supplemental book will walk you through these challenges and much more. When you've been back and forth through the pages of this book; when you've practised and refined the processes herein; when you remember the words you've read by heart, new knowledge is waiting for you to grasp it and run with it. For all you've put in, there's still more to get out. Consider advancing to the next book, and accelerating your new profession.

Conclusion

Congratulations! You've completed Property Investment Secrets - Rent to Rent: A Complete Property Investing Guide! I hope this journey has been an exciting and informative one and I thank you for travelling with me as your guide. As you've walked with me, you've gathered a true sense of what a rent-to-rent business looks like and how it operates legally, professionally, and ethically. This already puts you out ahead of the pack.

What's more, you've learned the importance of developing a 12-month business strategy and how to use this document regularly as you search for properties, negotiate with property owners, and sublet the units you manage. You're now familiar with the process of establishing and registering your business and the small but significant steps in that process which you cannot skip or else you leave yourself and your business open and unprotected from liability, fines, and even criminal prosecution. This puts you miles ahead of most individuals out there on their various paths, trying to eke out a fast and furious profit through subletting.

You now have in your tool kit a 5-step process for finding viable properties. Along with this process, you have a comprehensive breakdown of the means for negotiating with property owners and how to close those deals. You're prepared to walk into a viewing of the unit with all the questions and concerns that may arise, plus how to begin and complete the application process for tenants.

At the end of your first 12-month period, you exactly which aspects of your business to focus on for annual growth in the coming 12-month period and how to select the strategies that will work best for you. You understand that this is just the beginning and you have much to still learn from others and experience yourself, but the path to that excellence is clear. This puts you lightyears ahead of the rest.

From this point on, you can walk into the world of rent-to-rent with confidence and knowledge that many never gain and actually lose sight of as they try to keep from sinking in a business they did not prepare for. But not you. You're far-removed from this floundering and deep in the lead; staring at success; staring at a healthy profit and prosperity; staring right in the eyes of an expanding business set for greatness on the horizon.

Take what you've learned here and implement it without hesitation. Find the pieces you now know you need and lock them into place. Set out with one deliberate foot in front of the other on the heels of your next victory. Return to these lessons often and as you go, augment them to serve you best.

It's true that a successful sublet business can be yours. The dream of working for yourself and gaining greater control and fortune through this business model is real. It's within your grasp. Now reach out and take it.

A Short message from the Author:

Hey, did you enjoy reading this book? I'd love to hear your thoughts!

Many readers do not know how hard reviews are to come by, and how much they help a new author like myself. Reviews alone are what typically makes my book stand out in the crowd and persuades another person to choose this book.

I would be incredibly grateful if you could take just 60 seconds is all it takes to write a brief review (even if it's just a few sentences) on whatever bookstore or marketplace you purchased this book from!

Thank you for taking the time to share your thoughts!

RENT TO RENT
YOU'VE GOT QUESTIONS,
I'VE GOT ANSWERS!

Introduction

Congratulations on your purchase of *Rent to Rent: You've Got Questions, I've Got Answers* and welcome.

You've taken the next logical step in your rent-to-rent enterprise by investing in this guide to subletting. You may have already read my first book in the Property Investment Secrets series, *Rent to Rent: A Complete Rental Property Investment Guide.* Although my first book was laid out as a thorough step by step guide, I did receive some questions about topics I briefly skimmed over previously, so the answers will be included in detail within this book. Most people will read a book and then forget 80% of the content, so if you have any questions in the future, you can quickly refer to the contents page and locate them.

For Example:

- Who pays for renovations and updates to the property?
- What goes into a rent-to-rent contract?
- When should I outsource and hire contractors?
- Where do I look for available properties to manage?
- Why does the rent-to-rent business model fail for some people and work for others?
- How do I manage a small HMO (house in multiple occupation) renovation?

Establishing your own rent-to-rent business can pay off in the short and long term, but it requires attention, care, and knowledge. Gathered in these sister books, you'll find all the insider information you need to get started.

Rent to Rent: You've Got Questions, I've Got Answers has collected the crucial questions and organized them into a meaningful Q&A query format that's easy and efficient to access for fast answers as you move through the rent-to-rent real estate environment.

In this book, you'll find my most successful tips to make a significant profit with subletting, and break into the property investment profession quickly. You're about to see that subletting takes focus and time, but you can learn to grow money fast and build a legitimate business which will scale with you as new real estate investments approach.

I'll explain how to manage a small HMO renovation, which regulations you need to be aware of, the legal requirements and permissions necessary, and how to increase the value of a property with a few vital updates. I've included answers about starting a sublet business from scratch, how to market that business for success, and how to grow the business once it's reached a healthy cycle of profit generation.

By the time you've completed this book, you will have learned the foundation of creating an ethical rent-to-rent business. You've just selected a compilation that will take you from registering your new business to managing an HMO renovation, to conducting tenant screening, and growing through market strategy and self-development.

You've made the first decision which will impact positively on your success by learning from those who've already been there.

This book is for you if you've ever been curious about what it takes to start a rent-to-rent business or serious about starting one.

Use this book in conjunction with its predecessor *Rent to Rent: A Complete Rental Property Investment Guide.* Use them as your reference/support guide. Refer back to them as your textbooks. Don't be afraid to highlight relevant sections and make notes in the margins. Learn from them and come back to me with your questions and queries, and make the most of challenging opportunities to enable you to expand and dominate rent-to-rent.

Chapter 1:
Rent-to-Rent: A Basic Understanding

You've just purchased your ticket to the rent-to-rent drag races, and you're about to witness an incredible show. Some of these professionals have tricks of the trade and fancy techniques to get ahead fast with sublet investments. You're about to see how these pros go from 0 to 60 in split seconds and come out holding a handsome profit. The thrill of the ride will excite you and you'll wonder why you couldn't do it yourself.

Indeed, why not?

You have what it takes for rent-to-rent, don't you?

You have an insatiable desire to learn how others are doing it. You have the time to invest in this business goal. You're creative, resilient, and adaptable. You're passionate about the prize just over the finish line.

You know there's something to this, and if you could just crack it, you'd be on the other side; a slick professional with impressive techniques and a collection of trophies and winnings. The trophies are your HMOs and rental properties, and your winnings are the profits you make on each property after expenses are paid. You can crack it, and this book is your codebreaker.

Let's get a quick look at the tools we're working with, which will help to lay the foundations for the future. The answers to the questions in this section will get you up to speed fast on what rent-to-rent really is, and how it works. Whether you're new to subletting or you've been in the business for a while, this chapter is a practical review of the basics. When you're done with this section, you'll have gained an overall understanding of how rent-to-rent investment properties work and whether or not this race is for you. There's no shame in admitting this isn't your kind of game, but just think of what's possible over that finish line. Don't let fear drive you away from your goals and desires. As you move through these lessons, you'll build the confidence you need to 'put the pedal to the metal' when the green light says GO!

1. What is rent-to-rent?

You've likely heard the concept of *rent-to-own*; a tenant rents a residence from a landlord or property owner with the eventual intention of purchasing the residence. That tenant *rents-the-property-to-own-it*. In the case of *rent-to-rent*, the intention is to rent the residence from a landlord or property owner and then *sublet* that residence to another party which actually occupies the unit.

In an ideal situation, the renter does not live in the property with the subletter, but it's certainly possible. When the property being sublet is a multiple occupancy home, sometimes the renter will occupy one space, and the subletter will occupy another, within the same property. Your arrangement may perhaps begin this way, but as you accumulate income, you'll likely want to move out of that co-living space and into your own space. This also allows you to sublet the space you were living in, creating more profit.

Rent-to-rent doesn't necessarily mean residential space, though this is what we'll focus on for the most part. Some rent-to-rent professionals focus on commercial property, or property designed for short term accommodations; like Airbnb units, travel units, and holiday apartments. I find the most success by focusing on residential HMO properties (as opposed to single-family homes). These units tend to make money faster, and the business is easy to scale.

Whether you're a property owner, renter, or tenant, there are advantages that come with a proper rent-to-rent scenario. However, a rent-to-rent scenario that has not been established properly will come with a variety of disadvantages. As you move through the information in this book, you'll learn how to avoid those disadvantages and how to benefit from the proper rent-to-rent business setup.

2. Who is who in rent-to-rent?

To keep it simple, there are three major players in a sublet scenario:

The property owner is the person with exclusive rights and control over the property you rent; the lessor, the individual with the mortgage to the property; the individual who holds ownership of the property.

The renter is the person renting from the property owner - that's you! We commonly refer to the renter as the property manager, and sometimes as the landlord.

The subletter is the third party that rents the property from you at a higher price; the actual occupants of the property.

If you want to go beyond that, there are other key players in a rent-to-rent scenario, especially if it's an HMO property you operate. There's the local authority (council) whose regulations and requirements you must. There's the authorised consumer redress scheme, the health and safety regulators, insurance companies, and the mortgage companies. Sometimes additional banks and lenders. If you're managing a renovation or even repairs at any point, contractors are someone you'll see frequently.

3. How does rent-to-rent work?

Rent-to-rent, or subletting, is sometimes called "guaranteed rent", which refers to one of the biggest benefits of a rent-to-rent situation for the property owner. In a rent-to-rent agreement, the property owner typically agrees to a set rental price that may be a little lower than market value, but in return, the owner is guaranteed that you will deliver this rent each month, whether or not the rental unit is occupied, and whether or not the tenant has paid rent to you. Essentially, it removes some of the risks for the property owner and puts it on you. If the property owner can work with someone like you; motivated to make money, it's a better guarantee that they will be able to make the mortgage payment each month without worrying about tenants. In exchange, you're able to manage the property and thus charge tenants what you like (within reason).

For you, this translates to a better profit if you do your homework and manage the property effectively. You'll want to investigate the average rental rates, how long tenants tend to stay, and what the rental increase rates and rent control limits stipulate for the area. With this information, you can set a rental cost for the property that will pay the guaranteed rent, cover general property maintenance, and still give you a healthy profit each month.

For the property owner, this translates to a guaranteed rent that will cover the costs of the property, such as the mortgage, insurance, and any local taxes and fees. It also means the property owner will not necessarily need to find or pay for an agent to manage the rental property and there's still rent coming in even when the residence is vacant.

In most cases, the cost of any property upgrades and repairs is yours to bear as the party who manages the property. This includes ensuring all health and safety regulations are met within the property at the onset of subletting, and all of the maintenance henceforth. Before you finalise your agreement with your property owner, it's crucial to determine and document which party will be responsible for these costs - especially in the case of HMO properties; where the regulations are of particular importance.

In terms of process, subletting works in a predominantly straightforward way. You start by doing research on locations you're familiar with that would make for a good rent-to-rent investment opportunity. With a couple of potential areas in mind, you can then search for potential properties. At this point, you'll start to speak with, and negotiate with the property owners. With the right agreement signed between you and the property owner, you now have a property to manage. Either the property already has tenants in it, or you need to fill it. In either case, you'll need to make sure that the building is up to code and that it's occupied and making money. From that point, it's about proper management of tenants and care for the property.

Each month, your tenant(s) pay the rent you've set, and you pay the property owner the guaranteed rent. As you gain income, you may choose to invest in more properties, in which case, you begin the process again.

4. Is subletting illegal?

In short, no; subletting is not illegal. It's perfectly legal, unless you conduct your business improperly and you don't adhere to regulations. Three cardinal rules will ensure your rent-to-rent operation is legitimate: (1) the sublet operation must be legal and transparent in all ways, and (2) the property must fulfil all requirements and regulations set forth on a local or national level. (3) It is permissible if the initial agreement prohibits subletting, so the contracts you use are crucial!

Be transparent. Subletting shouldn't be something sneaky you're getting away with, it should be managed properly and agreed to by all parties. First and foremost, you should have an agreement with the property owner, that you plan to sublet the space. Further, that agreement should be in writing. Typically, rental contracts between the property owner and tenant stipulate that the property cannot be sublet. In other cases, the contract between the property owner and tenant may make no mention of subletter whatsoever; leaving doubt as to whether that makes subletting legal. It does not. Just because a rental agreement doesn't outright say you cannot sublet, it doesn't mean you can. For the most transparent and simplest solution, be upfront in your discussions with the property owner and absolutely make sure the rental agreement contains a statement indicating it's agreeable to sublet.

Transparency with the property owner is the first step, but you'll also need to be transparent with the mortgage and insurance providers. Unless the property is owned already, it is likely to have a mortgage attached to it. That mortgage lender may include as part of their terms and conditions that subletting is not allowed for the property being mortgaged. This is sometimes the case because lenders feel that creating a space (like an HMO) where the traffic and wear-and-tear on the property will be increased is too risky. Thus, they limit against it. Insurance providers may contain a similar stipulation in their terms and conditions for the same reasons. Before finalising your rent-to-rent agreement with the property owner, verify that the terms and conditions from both the mortgage lender and the insurance provider will not impede your subletting operation. Operating around the mortgage lender and insurance provider, without transparency, puts you at risk - actually it puts both you and the property owner at risk. The consequences for operating without transparency can mean the loss of the mortgage, the loss of insurance coverage, fines, and probably the swift end to subletting now and at any time in the future.

Once you've made it clear that you intend to sublet, you have one more critical step for managing a legal sublet operation: ensure the property is regulation ready. Depending on whether the property is an AST (assured shorthold tenancy) or an HMO (house of multiple occupancy), you'll find a set of rules and regulations that are important for you to follow, both in how you conduct your business and how the property is physically equipped and secured. In short, as the manager of the property, there are business and legal responsibilities to uphold. If that property is an HMO, there are additional business and legal responsibilities to uphold. For example, a property operating as an HMO must be registered as such, whereas an AST property likely will not need any additional registration.

Above all, there are health and safety regulations to uphold, and again, if that property is an HMO, you'll find the regulations a bit stricter and more thorough, simply because more individuals living in a given space increases the risk of a hazard in that space.

5. What are the risks of subletting?

The number one risk of subletting is that you can be exposed to some serious and important expenses. Every month, whether or not you collect rent on time from your subletters, you must pay the property owner guaranteed rent. Even if the accommodation is empty, you must pay the agreed-upon price for guaranteed rent. In addition, in most cases, all renovations, updates, and maintenance are probably at your expense. Some of these projects are crucial for an HMO property and will need to be completed before tenants live in it. How to afford these updates and renovations is almost always a responsibility and expense the property manager must withstand. If you're going to furnish the accommodation, that's an expense to you, too, and you run the risk of that property being destroyed and needing replacement.

As part of a rent-to-rent scheme, you don't own the property, so you make a significant financial investment into the updates and maintenance of the property, but you never see anything for capital return; that's the property owner.

On the other hand, as a renter and not the property owner, you're not responsible for the payment of any stamp duty or property conveyancing costs, mortgages, and perhaps insurance costs for the property.

6. What is an HMO?

Before we go further, let's define what is, and is not an HMO property. There are three common types of rent-to-rent properties that you'll regularly encounter: HMOs, ASTs, and commercial properties. We'll start backwards with what an HMO is *not*:

Commercial properties are non-residential spaces rented out for business. Depending on the location and the opportunities, it might be a wise idea to invest in commercial real estate rather than residential, but I find the need for residential rentals ever-increasing in the areas in which I work and thus I stick with the demand and what I know best. Commercial properties come with their own unique set of rules and regulations when it comes to health and safety. Though many of these are similar to the regulations of a residential space, if you're dealing in commercial space, become conversant with all relevant requirements. Commercial properties are not HMOs.

ASTs, or assured shorthold tenancies, are traditionally the most common kind of residential property rental. These properties are occupied by only one household for an agreed leasing period of usually 6 months or a year, at the end of which a new agreement must be signed. ASTs are very commonly private rentals and do not necessarily require a business registration. The health and safety regulations for an AST differ slightly from an HMO. Again, it's important to become conversant with the requirements and parameters you'll be expected to follow. Knowing these requirements inside out can make a world of difference and save you thousands in your ongoing investment. ASTs are not HMOs.

HMOs are "houses in multiple occupation". These properties are sometimes also referred to as "house shares". Basically, more than one household lives within the same dwelling. In an HMO residence, some of the living space and facilities are shared between households, such as the kitchen and bathroom facilities, laundry facilities, and outdoor facilities. In most locations, an HMO is defined by three or more individuals living in the same residence, but under separate households; in some areas, it's five or more individuals. HMOs are similar to ASTs in that very often there's an agreement signed between you and the tenant for 6 months or a year, at the end of which a new agreement is signed or the tenant is replaced. In some cases, HMOs might be intended for shorter periods of stay. Such as in accommodation-style properties rented out to holidaymakers, company representatives, and students staying only a few weeks or months.

If you'll be renting out your property as an HMO, this requires you to register the property as such with your local council. By officially recognising and registering the property as an HMO, you are now responsible for ensuring that it's equipped and managed in accordance with local and national HMO regulations. Each HMO registration is only good for that specific property, and each HMO must be registered separately. HMO licencing expires every five years.

I encourage you to search for the requirements in your specific area. You can apply for registration online (at the Gov.uk website) by postcode, which will also outline all of the parameters and regulations for HMOs in your area. Failure to register properly will result in fines, legal issues, the cessation of your business operation, and possibly even imprisonment. Don't take the chance.

7. Why does the rent-to-rent model fail for some?

Overall, there's a very damaging misconception about rent-to-rent which gives the impression that it's a set-and-forget operation. Subletting is not easy, and it's not for everyone. It takes a certain kind of personality and drive to run a subletting business effectively. Some individuals start out with some investment capital while others do not. Managing the property requires time and care that some individuals already don't have enough of, so the property and the tenants suffer. These are the biggest factors I see when comparing successful rent-to-rent operations to the failed ones.

First and foremost, rent-to-rent business is like any other growing business. It needs to be nurtured to grow; it's not a turn-key operation, even if the property is a turn-key property. There are constant obligations as with any business. Give yourself a realistic expectation from the start; you will need to invest time and energy into this business if it's to grow and become a lasting success. If you think you're going to sublet a property and let things take care of themselves, you're headed toward being a slumlord; obviously not a successful enterprise.

A property and the tenants within it must be taken care of, protected, and maintained in accordance with laws and regulations. Ensuring compliance, documenting records, maintaining the property, and managing the tenants must all be done with genuine care. Rushing through these processes will cost you in the long run. If you do not, for example, vet prospective tenants before subletting to them, you risk inviting untrustworthy individuals into your business opportunity. If you do not, for example, market a vacancy and fill it swiftly, you will lose profit repeatedly until you do. These are just examples of work that requires time and energy to do it right.

This kind of work isn't for everyone. You generally need to be an assertive individual that takes the initiative and demonstrates drive and enthusiasm; a people-person, hands-on, and not so much the man behind the scene. If you're not willing to be aggressive, consistent, and self-managed, you might not be cut out for this type of business.

Lastly, I see a fair amount of failures and successes in ventures that start with investment capital and those that do not. Money to invest definitely helps; I won't lie. But I should say that I tend to see operations thrive more quickly when they are careful and deliberate about expenses. Sometimes when your budget is limited, it forces you to analyse business decisions better. If you're starting out with some investment capital, consider yourself lucky, but don't take it for granted.

8. How fast can I make a profit?

How fast you can make a profit is dictated by multiple factors which change with any given scenario. Rather than tell you exactly has fast you can expect to make a profit, allow me to explain the major factors that will determine how long it takes to start making a profit. Simply put, what are your expenses going to look like for the property you have in mind? Consider the entire picture.

Depending on the type of opportunity you pursue, or how far along in your business process you are, you may run into business start-up costs. If you're just starting up, you'll likely need to register your business and open the associated business banking account. You might need to pay for business insurance, redress scheme membership, taxes, and various minor business expenses. If your business has employees, you'll definitely need to consider national Insurance taxes and employee rights and benefits, even in the case of freelance contractors in some cases. Business expenses are a peripheral cost that is often overlooked in the beginning. Neglecting these figures will cut into your estimated time and profit.

Probably the most significant expense will be preparing a property to meet all the health and safety requirements demanded of you in your specific location. If you're subletting an HMO as opposed to an AST, these requirements can be even more stringent. It may require you to install new fire and emergency equipment, or even require a small renovation to ensure safe and accessible exits from the unit in the case of an emergency. Whatever the case, these expenses will have an effect on when your profit begins.

Consistent property management is also an expense you more than likely bear as the renter and property manager. If appliances break it's up to you to replace them. If plumbing or electrical issues arise, it's your responsibility to have them repaired. These expenses are difficult to foresee, so it's a smart idea to hold part of the income you collect so that when these issues to arise, you can squash them quickly.

Now consider what you're paying to the property owner as guaranteed monthly rent, and what you'll be collecting in rental fees from tenants. A broad and simple figure to keep in mind is half; half of what you collect in rent will be used for monthly expenses and payments. This, of course, will vary from circumstance to circumstance, but it's a fair benchmark.

So, now that you've figured into the equation business costs, renovation costs, maintenance and marketing, and the guaranteed rent you pay, you can determine how long it will take you to be clear of any investments to repair or renovate the property and so forth. In some cases, a loan might be taken out in order to cover the expenses of renovation. Making a smaller monthly payment for these renovations may drag your timeline out a bit further on your profit, but it can be more manageable in the end.

The point here, really, is that there's no exact answer on how fast you can make a profit. It depends entirely on the circumstances in any given scenario. Compare your expenses to the total you collect from subletters to determine how fast you'll be paid off and how quickly you'll be making a strong profit with minimal expense.

9. Can I do this with no money to invest?

Yes, in theory, you can sublet a rent-to-rent property from day one without investing a drop of money. Realistically, however, investing a small amount of money can make your process easier and faster, and ultimately more successful. If you have absolutely no money to invest, it means you probably can't register a property as an HMO, you probably cannot register your business or open a business banking account, you probably cannot afford to make repairs or renovations yet, and you probably can afford to market and showcase the unit for occupancy. This puts many restrictions on you, but it doesn't make it impossible. It means you have to be extremely careful and deliberate in your hunt for the right property and agreement. It means you need to pay close attention to your business plan, especially in the beginning, when making money to invest back into the property will be very important.

It's not unusual for an individual starting out with no investment capital to begin with a single unit to rent to a single tenant. The income raised from this for a few months provides enough money to start taking care of the steps in the process that were unaffordable at the time, such as registering as a business, registering as an HMO, or having renovations done to the property. With these steps taken care of, the one tenant becomes multiple and the profit increases. Just remember, if you've taken out a loan or something similar to cover the cost of renovations, this payment will be an added monthly expense to include in your bottom line.

10.   Do I have what it takes to succeed with Rent-to-Rent?

Now you've started to get an overview of what's involved in building a rent-to-rent business. This isn't the kind of business you can "set and forget" with the expectation that it will operate on its own and generate a profit. This business is not passive- at least yet. You'll need to be involved in your start-up on probably a daily basis in one respect or another.

Time can be the most difficult requirement to fill, especially if your rent-to-rent business is a side business. Time is one ingredient you will need at the start, like it or not. If you don't find some time to dedicate to the enterprise, it will never be a business; just a side project. You'll need to make time to get the business going, plan your strategy and business goals, negotiate, market your unit, and to manage your tenants and space. If you're hoping to grow quickly, you need additional time to accomplish this with more than one unit. You may already be confident in your ability to manage your time properly, but here are a few tips to keep in mind as you begin:

Prioritise what needs to be done first or with utmost urgency. For example, getting a business licence would be a priority, but setting up an online presence can happen later in the game. Break large tasks into smaller tasks you can accomplish in about an hour or two. All of the steps in front of you can seem daunting, but if you break them into smaller steps, they are more manageable throughout your day or your week.

Don't guess at what's next to be done; make yourself a business roadmap. Outline all the steps you need to take to get one subletter into a unit under your rent-to-rent business and mark out on your calendar or diary when you need them to be complete. Allow for adjustments in the roadmap.
Avoid time-wasting activities and time-wasting individuals when you can. Interruptions are inevitable, but you'll have to get a bit selfish with your time, and you should not feel guilty about it.

Delegate when you can. But keep in mind if you delegate a few steps to another individual, chances are you'll need to compensate them monetarily. For example, if you're focused on setting up a Google Ad for your units, this might be better delegated to someone who already knows how to set this up. You can often find professional virtual assistants to help you on sites like Fiverr.com or Freelancer.com. These tasks can usually be completed at a very low rate because many of the freelance workers on these sites are international and work for a lower cost per hour or per job than you might find in your own neighbourhood. Though these tasks would be outsourced, the quality of the work remains acceptable because these virtual assistants regularly perform these tasks and understand what's expected despite not being local. If even a low monetary compensation is not in your budget, you can often find free apps and programs that automate parts of your business process. Take time-consuming tasks off of your list and put them onto the lists of robots or other professionals via delegation.

Don't cancel appointments on yourself. When you put a task into your diary, but there's no one else to be accountable to, it's very easy to cancel on yourself. Don't. Think of a time when you may have put into your diary an appointment with yourself to go to the gym in the morning. When the alarm goes off, and you're still sleepy, and no one is waiting for you to show up, it's pretty easy to turn the alarm off and roll back into your warm sheets. Don't allow this to happen with the self-appointments you set for your rent-to-rent business. Though you might not have a direct person to be accountable to other than yourself, there are ways to prompt your own accountability. Search for free apps that help you to stay on task and accountable. Better yet, use social media to find yourself a mastermind group to join for entrepreneurs, or even more specifically, property management entrepreneurs. These kinds of support groups often have accountability processes built in because you're definitely not the only one facing this challenge. If you know you'll have to report back to your mastermind group with the results of the day, you may be more apt to do them.

It's going to be crucial for you to set tasks and goals for yourself and your business and take responsibility for their completion. Even if you delegate tasks to others, you are still the one ultimately responsible for them. This is why it's a good idea to seek out an online application (like Asana) that will keep you on task. A tool like this will make your business life much easier. I don't have to worry about losing paper notes to myself or wonder what I need to do next, because the app tells me every day what's on my to-do list. You can even make your business roadmap inside this tool. Set dates, hold all of your project documentation and links there; it really does everything you need.

Things aren't always going to go your way, and people aren't always going to do what you want, but it's important to keep your composure. Your body language is very revealing whether you're aware of it or not. Your posture, gestures, facial expressions, and breathing are all telling others what you're thinking and feeling even if your words aren't saying it. If you're not already familiar with how to use these aspects of yourself to communicate deliberately, then it's worth a brush-up. Though you may not feel confident negotiating and signing your very first deal, you want to give the impression you are. Believe it or not, these methods of communication can make or break your deal. Studies reveal that over fifty per cent of an individual's first impression and opinion of another is based on body language and appearance alone. Only about five per cent of an individual's impression of another is based on the words and verbal language communicated.

When you interact with prospective property owners and tenants, be cognisant of your posture. Stand straight with your shoulders back. Make eye contact. Smile. When they nod, you nod. Take notice of whether your shoulders are squarely facing the prospect or whether they are turned away. The same principle goes for the direction your feet are facing. If your shoulders and feet are facing an exit, for example, it gives the subconscious impression that you're looking for a way out; an escape.

If you start to get nervous, practise a slow and steady breath through your nose during your interaction. It's said that the person in the room with the most control is the one with a steady and calm breath. These practices may not come naturally at first, but give them some practice in other areas of your life.

Beyond your own physical and verbal communication is theirs. Pay attention to the other person's cues for insight into how they're feeling and what they're thinking. This can help you build a rapport with them, and even anticipate their questions and decisions.

Plans change all the time; priorities shift; deadlines change. You almost have to expect it and be ready to pivot your plan as needed so you will not slow your momentum. Make a business plan and roadmap for yourself but don't be afraid to update it at any time. Holding tight to a rigid plan with no room for change is the weakness. It can actually be a sign of strong business to change and adapt regularly. It's a demonstration of your drive and mastery to be able to amend plans and bounce back when things change, not to mention an understanding of the market.

Continuously put yourself in new learning situations. Join online or in-person webinars, seminars, and classes. Find a mentor. There are plenty of ways to ensure you're always learning about the industry and its technologies, philosophies, developments, and best practices.

If you can embrace these traits, you have a strong and winning chance of being the kind of person who has what it takes to operate and rent-to-rent business successfully.

11.   What are the regulations?

In general, there are three major sets of regulations to keep abreast with. Though these will vary from specific circumstance to circumstance, you'll almost always have to comply with business regulations, health and safety regulations, and local regulations. We'll go into each of these in more detail in their respective sections, but it's important to recognise these three broad categories of regulation you'll be working with. Each of these sets of regulations are crucial to operating a legitimate subletting business. I highly advise learning the regulations and adhering to them. Penalty for ignoring any of these sets of regulations will result in fines and the cessation of your business operation, not to mention the very real possibility of imprisonment, depending on how severely you've neglected regulations. Don't cut corners here; follow the rules.

Chapter 2:

Contracts and Requirements

At this point, you've got a solid idea of what you're working with. You understand who is responsible for what, what's legal and illegal, the rules and regulations of the game, and what to expect. Now it's time to approach the starting line and gain traction.

In rent-to-rent, this looks like getting a grip on contract specifics. The rental contract you use with property owners can differ depending on the property itself, how it will operate, who is responsible for what, and at what cost. The contracts you use with tenants are arguably even more important. If you use the wrong kind of agreement, it can be a nightmare to remove lingering tenants.

In this section, you'll gain an insight into the types of contracts you'll commonly run into, and what's important to include in each of them. We'll also prepare you for the regulations and obligations you can expect as part of the everyday rent-to-rent business.

By the end of this section, you have the knowledge you need to start the race, and when the time comes to negotiate and sign with prospects, you're ahead of the mark; able to move swiftly when you get there because you've already laid the necessary groundwork.

12.   How do contracts differ for each property model?

The AST agreement is the most common type of contract used between the renter (you) and the subletter (tenant). In most cases, an Assured Shorthold Tenancy (AST) agreement will be sufficient, even in some HMO scenarios. An AST agreement between you and the individual(s) subletting is a contract to set clearly the terms and conditions of renting the property. An AST agreement can be used if you're subletting to one individual or household that will be occupying the entire unit.

You can also use an AST agreement if you have multiple tenants or households within the same property - *except if* you yourself are not one of the tenants within that property. If you are also a tenant of that property, you should use an "excluded tenancy" agreement which is intended for lodgers. When you also live in the property you sublet, your tenants are technically lodgers. This makes a big difference to you because if your lodgers/tenants have an AST agreement, it's a much harder process for you to remove them and in general they have more rights. In real terms, this could mean saving yourself and your investment from untrustworthy tenants taking advantage of your property and staying without paying. An AST protects the tenant more so than an excluded tenancy. Additionally, you will not be required to protect yourself and your tenants with a redress scheme or a Tenancy Deposit Protection Scheme, which would absolutely be required in the case of an AST contract. If your model is to operate a property that caters to AirBnB guests, travellers, and students or professionals staying only a short time (less than 6 months), the lodger model is for you.

While an AST agreement can be used for many scenarios, the following cases are examples of when this type of agreement will *not* be the proper contract for you and your tenants:

- If the tenancy began prior to 1997
- If the property belongs to the government or the Crown
- If the property earns over 100k annually in rent
- If the property receives £250 or less annually in rent
- If the property is a holiday dwelling
- If the property contains two or more acres of agricultural land
- If the property is being rented to a company rather than an individual

If your tenants began renting the property prior to 1997, or if the property is rented by an association rather than an individual, you're likely to find the contract is an "Assured Tenancy" (rather than an Assured Shorthold Tenancy). The major difference between the two is the legal process one must follow in order to remove tenants from the property. If the property is being rented to a company or business rather than an individual or household, then a "Company Let" will be the appropriate contract between you and your tenants.

If you're in the start-up phases of your rent-to-rent business, I'd recommend avoiding the less common scenarios with curious stipulations and requirements, but if you insist and you're still unsure as to the proper contracts to use between you and your tenant, don't guess; check. Visit gov.uk for the final word in what to use and how to use it.

13. What should my contract look like for my tenants?

Let's assume the most common and preferable property model, in my opinion, and say for the sake of example that you are now subletting an HMO-style property that accommodates three individuals. We'll say further, that your residence is separate from these accommodations, so you're not using a lodger model; you're using the HMO property model and you're ready to utilize AST agreements between you and your tenants.

When making an agreement between you and your tenants, it's important to be clear and specific; don't cut corners or make assumptions. Include details on every rule and expectation you can, so that both parties are understanding and agreeing to the same clear terms.

Since your ideal example property accommodates three individuals, I recommend subletting to three separate people and not necessarily three friends. In either case, I recommend creating an agreement between you and each one of the tenants individually, rather than include all three people on one agreement. In the first place, it will make life easier for you as tenants come and go, but it also provides the clearest version of who is expected to do what. Further, in the unfortunate case of legal action, it will be much easier for you to pursue individual AST contracts.

A side note about renting to friends versus strangers: while you'll have to make that final decision with your own information and instinct, in general, three separate individuals is safer for you as the renter and property manager. Three friends will likely all move at the same time and instead of a hit to one stream of income, it's a hit to all three for you. The dynamic between co-habitants that aren't friends first, tends to be cordial and respectful to one another and to the property. Three friends living together may have some benefits, but I've seen the personal relationships get in the way of financial obligations, and I've seen the deterioration of property take place faster with friends, perhaps because the attitude and sentiment are already so casual and informal between the friends.

So we'll say you have three AST agreements; one for each of your tenants. This is what you should be sure to include:

Indication of the date of the agreement, the signing, and the length of the tenancy; the date the tenancy is over. As a tip, write out the entire date; for example, 01/12/20 should be written December 01, 2020, or 01 December 2020. Writing the full date leaves no room for error or misinterpretation. AST agreements typically last for 6 months or one year, at which time a new contract is signed for the next period of time.

Indication of the amount of rent that will be due each month, the day or date it will regularly be due, and the penalties to be applied in the case of late or unpaid rent.
Indication of the tenant's responsibilities for the care of the property and its appliances and resources. In most cases, this is a very minimal responsibility. For example, the tenant often agrees to the replacement of any light bulbs as needed, or a tenant might agree to the upkeep of a yard in exchange for the okay to plant what he or she likes and decorate the space according to their own liking.

Indication of what will be expected of the tenant in terms of noise and annoyances that may provoke cohabitants or neighbours. If you visit gov.uk you can find the rules and regulations on noise, pets, pests, and building and renovation in your local area.

The condition that the property is used for residential purposes only; that no business will be run out of the property, especially such that would warrant foot-traffic and the coming and going of clients or customers.

The condition that no pet can be kept on the property without written permission. Keep in mind that if you do permit pets, you may be entitled to collect an additional fee for that. The additional pet fee would help to mitigate any accidental or intentional damage done to the property as a result of keeping the pet on the property.

The condition that the property should not be left alone and unattended for a maximum length of time (21 days is common) without informing you.

The condition that additional visitors are not allowed, or allowed only for a maximum period of time (overnight, three days, one week).

The indication of which changes, if any, are allowed to be made to the property while renting. This might include the changing of appliances, electrical work, changing locks, painting or renovating, changing floors or ceilings, and so forth.

One of the most important expectations to be set in the AST contract between you and each tenant is who will be responsible for additional costs such as utilities. If you're able to afford it, I highly recommend keeping the major utilities in your name and paying them yourself. Even utilities like phone, internet, and cable can be kept in your name and provided as a part of the accommodations. As a result, you're able to reasonably increase the rental cost for each tenant in order to cover the cost of these accommodations. This also saves the inevitable hassle of switching over utilities, which can be a constant nuisance to the productivity of your business. Whether you keep bills in your name or assign them to tenants, make sure that each contract is clear in which utilities the tenant is responsible for paying for and what percentage.

Another important note in the case of an AST agreement: for each AST agreement you sign with a tenant, you are required to join an authorized Tenancy Deposit Protection scheme which properly protects the tenant's deposit upon moving into the property. If a deposit is taken and no tenancy deposit protection is joined within 14 days, you'll be subject to fines and legal prosecution.

14. What should I know about property mortgages and insurance policies?

If your business is rent-to-rent, it's safe for us to assume for the sake of example that the property you'll be subletting is neither yours nor the property owner. It is likely the property owner pays a mortgage on the property and rents it to you. In the case that the property is not owned outright and does indeed have a mortgage, then it's important to check the terms and conditions of that mortgage. It may be against the lender's terms and conditions to sublet HMO-style, for example. You'll have to find some way to work within the parameters of the terms and conditions of the mortgage or consider working with another mortgage lender, or property. If you think you can sneak by these rules, know that if you're caught, it could not only mean fines and legal issues for both you and the property owner, but the property could be taken from the owner, in which case you might be looking at some pretty serious legal issues. At best.

The same care and consideration should be taken with the insurance for the property. Make sure there are no terms and conditions from the insurance provider that would prevent you from operating as a rental, or HMO. In some cases, the insurance lender's terms and conditions will prohibit a residence from operating as a house of multiple occupancy because it can pose greater risks to the property itself, or the safety of others on the property. Again, you may think you can wiggle around this condition, but you risk not being covered should anything go wrong, and you risk losing your insurance policy altogether.

15. What obligations do I have for tenant viewings and applications?

There are two keys to keep in mind when viewing the property with prospective tenants, when conducting the pre-screening and screening processes, and when signing the agreement: discrimination and information.

Avoid anything that can be construed as discrimination at any point in the subletting process. There are a few simple practices you can employ to ensure you're operating without discrimination.

Foremost, you're required to show every prospective tenant all of the spaces to which they will have access. If the tenant can access the space during occupancy, then it needs to be part of the viewing.

Steering is a form of discrimination. Steering is when the landlord steers the prospective tenant toward or away from areas of the rental that should be shown. For example, steering a woman away from the attic, basement, electrical, or otherwise, with the assumption that she would not have an interest in that, is discrimination. Steering a disabled individual away from a balcony or stairwell that's not particularly handicap accessible is another example of discrimination. Show everything and show it to everyone, in the same order.

Next, create a process and stick to it. Do everything in the same order, for every prospective tenant, and don't skip a step for anyone. When you pre-screen, ask every prospective tenant the same questions. When you screen and do checks, don't skip any steps. When viewing the property with prospective tenants, give everyone the same information and documentation for the property and tenancy rights, etc. When you join a redress scheme, they often supply you with pamphlets you can and should give to prospective tenants about their rights and other transparent and helpful information.

In fact, information is the second key to keep in mind. This means giving everyone the same information and truly protecting their information. As part of GDPR compliance, for example, businesses like yours are expected to protect the personal information of tenants and prospective tenants after you've collected it. This could be how you store personal information, how you use it, if and when you delete it, and how you share it across your business. You can find more on GDPR compliance at the European Commission website.

From marketing materials to pamphlets, to contracts, all tenants and prospective tenants should be given the same documentation. When you've finally signed an AST agreement with your tenant, be sure that you each have a copy of the exact same contract, signed by each of you.

There's one more curveball when it comes to discrimination and information in the viewing process of your sublet management. Occupants. If you're showing a property to prospective tenants while there's still current tenants living in the space, it can get awkward. It's not ideal, but if you have to do it, you need to be respectful to the household; provide ample notice that the property will be shown. Try to show the property when it's convenient for the current resident. If you have current tenants, consider showing your appreciation for their cooperation in the form of a gift certificate or something similar.

16.   What Insurances do I need?

First and foremost, if you're operating an HMO property, you should acquire business insurance as part of your business setup. If you're operating an AST property, you don't necessarily need business insurance, but it doesn't hurt to have it, and it can certainly help. However, an HMO property should be registered as an HMO property, and your business should be a registered business of some type, other than a sole trader; limited companies being the most common choice. This means you'll need to have business insurance. Further, if you have employees, you're required by law to have employers' liability insurance. If your business includes vehicles registered as company vehicles, you're required by law to have commercial motor insurance on those vehicles. In addition, you'll want to consider commercial property insurance (depending on your office accommodations and the property being rented), and liability insurance, of which there are several to select from depending on what you need and want.

Beyond business insurance, you'll need to have insurance for the property itself being rented. If you're an AST operating a single unit, you can protect yourself and your property with landlord's insurance.

Operating an HMO property, or an accommodation property, will require something different. HMO landlord insurance is specifically for the insurance and protection of houses of multiple occupancy. The terms of HMO landlord insurance and somewhat different from standard landlord insurance. In the eyes of insurance providers, operating an HMO brings with it a higher risk for any of a variety of damages or losses, because of conditions such as regularly changing residents and heavily used common areas. HMO landlord insurance will also protect you in the unfortunate event of damage from water, fire, and storms, and both accidental and malicious damages from tenants in the same way standard landlord insurance does. You can also opt to protect included furnishings on the property, and even cover tenant losses, which can be an extra bonus to subletters that allows you to increase your final rental price.

If you operate multiple HMOs check with your specialist provider about insuring them on one policy. There are several benefits to this, including saving money on policies.

17.   What should my contract look like for my property owners?

The contract between you and the property owner should be clear about who is responsible for what. Again, you want to leave as little room as possible for error or misinterpretation. This contract should address two major components of the agreement: guaranteed rent and property management. It should almost go without saying – but definitely say it – that the property is intended to be sublet by you and under your management.

Before everything else, the contract should make it evident that the property owner intends to rent to you, and that you will in turn sublet. Specify which spaces will be sublet and any key tenancy terms and conditions that might apply to your situation. It also won't hurt to specify who is responsible for checking the terms and conditions of the mortgage and insurance policies for violations of operation and to verify that they've done so.

Next, indicate the guaranteed rent agreement and the total rental cost you'll be paying each month to the property owner in exchange for management and sublet control. Be sure to indicate when the agreement begins and ends.

Then you'll want to include the terms and conditions of property management. This should clarify what can and cannot be done to the property, parameters and regulations either party should not stray from, and who pays for what. Specify who is responsible for paying the mortgage, insurance, council tax, local fees, renovations, repairs, maintenance and upkeep, and utilities.

Lastly, include any other critical agreements between you and the property owner in the contract. The same way you would with a tenant, provide identical copies for yourself and the property owner; both signed by each of you.

Chapter 3:

Target Locations

Yellow light - yellow light - yellow light - green light! It's time to slam on the accelerator and start your fast and furious dash to the finish line.

In this section, we'll take a quick look at how to seek and find the best locations for rental investments. You'll learn what makes a good HMO location and the criteria I suggest using to compare locations for the best potential. Even if you're using a property model other than an HMO, I'll show you what's important to look for in any rent-to-rent location.

You don't want to select a location arbitrarily; there's a lot that goes into determining which areas will be successful for your business to start out. You want something easy enough to get to when you need to be there in person, but also you want a location that shows promise and a healthy economy, especially when it comes to real estate and rentals.

Next, we jump ahead in a short spurt to gain an understanding of how to find the best location near you to start looking for properties. Rev your engines - let's go!

18.   How do I select a location for an HMO?

Find three attractive locations that are nearby enough for you to reach easily. Reach profitable zones that are nearby and convenient enough for you to reach when you have to. When you do the research on each of these areas of interest, look for signs that the area is affluent or up-and-coming. You probably want locations with a higher average rental cost, unless one of your goals is to better communities through property management. Consider your ideal tenant and then search areas that these types of individuals are likely to be attracted to as their residence. It the location perhaps even a place you would consider living?

Investigate the following for each location:

- Average annual household income
- Average cost of buying a home
- Average mortgage rates
- Average rental cost
- Tax history
- Average tenant turnover rates
- Rise in home values
- Rise in rental values
- Job availability
- Unemployment rates
- Nearby school systems and ratings
- Nearby universities and ratings
- Public transportation
- Public resources
- Crime rates
- Utilities access and average costs

When you've found three locations that are worthy of your time, start searching for properties there.

19.   What makes a good location for an HMO?

As you become more proficient with your rent-to-rent experiences, you'll likely develop your own set of data you can't live without when you're making property location decisions. Until then, use these basic standards to determine if a location is worth searching for HMO property opportunities.

First, consider the population of the location. Which spots have a higher density than others? Which spots have been increasing or decreasing in interest in the last few years? Find a heatmap of the location and recognise trends that will be beneficial to utilise or avoid.

Next, determine the market activity for the area. Get a sense of the demand for HMO-style living spaces and how many exist currently or are being built. If the supply of co-living residences is short in an area where the demand has just increased, you can be at the head of filling a deep residential need in this location. This brings us to the final critical details to check: the competition. Find out how long the local competition has been operating. Check them out online. Browse the properties they manage and check out online reviews. Get to know them at networking events. Sometimes the competition can become your strongest ally.

20. What do I look for in a location if I'm not doing an HMO property?

Whether you're looking for an HMO property or another property model, you still need to keep the same key ideas in mind when searching for the right location. You'll need to study the market activity in that area and compare it to your business plan to find what will fit. If you're searching for an AST with one household only in the property, you'll still need to know the same information: get a sense for the population in the area and what kind of rentals are needed, and in short supply.

If your property model is for lodgers, you'll want to make sure it is fit for purpose. Firstly, you'll be searching for areas that have a high rate of traffic. Look for areas that see a lot of holidaymakers and tourists. Or, search for places near business complexes or schools and universities. These areas see a good deal of short-term tenancy or lodging from travellers, students, and professionals. You'll still want to keep an eye on market trends in the area to get a fair sense of what you can legitimately charge for such a unit. Just as you would any property model, you want to do your own market research to check out the competition.

21. How do I find local rental statistics and market insight?

On first thought, it may seem daunting to research and gather housing and rental statistics from the target locations you've selected. In reality, it's not difficult; it just takes a bit of time and concentration. If you're lucky enough to have an assistant, this might be an excellent task for them. With the statistics collected, you can view the report your assistant has generated and make informed decisions about which area is best for your next rent-to-rent investment.

It's important to remember than when you're collecting statistics for your target location(s), it's not just rental data alone you're interested in. To get a comprehensive view and sense for the location, investigate general housing statistics for the area in addition to rental activity. Go beyond that and collect general economic information for the area, too. If you collect the same set of statistics for each location, you'll easily be able to compare and knock your targets down to one prime location for your next opportunity. Where to look may seem daunting as well, but I assure you it's simple. There are several trustworthy places from which to gather this information.

You can find available properties and local housing statistics on sites like Zoopla, Home.co.uk, and OnTheMarket. If you want statistics that are less about the individual properties and more about the general estate agency economics for a given location, then I suggest visiting the Office for National Statistics, or Gov.UK for the most recent set of housing and rental market trends per area. These statistics can be extremely comprehensive, but they will be especially helpful as a deciding factor for location. If you're starting your rent-to-rent enterprise with little to no capital, these statistics will be of particular importance to you, as every detail serves to save you money, short-term and long-term, while still meeting your business goals. If your property model operates as a holiday unit or short-term rental (less than six months) for visiting students and professionals, AirDNA provides a comprehensive set of rental information for these lodger property models.

If you're at the point in your business plan when it makes sense to invest in software to help you better manage your rent-to-rent investments, there are a wide variety of online dashboards and tools at your disposal, for a price. Services like Hometrack, and competitors like PropertyData offer historical and predictive analytics for real estate consumers and professionals. These paid services help businesses like yours to keep an eye on vital statistics in any of your areas, in real-time. They generally offer a myriad of other tools and services in addition to the main data aggregation and reporting. If you're at the point where you need to keep track of multiple areas of investment, and multiple rent-to-rent properties, and you expect to continue growing, it may be time to consider investing in automation software like this to make your life easier and your decisions clear.

If you feel that this is too daunting, prioritising "what" to gather is probably the best thing to do until you get the hang of it. It's not the facts themselves; it's the insight you derive from them, so you want statistics that give you a comprehensive view or sense of the area. Look for information like estimated costs to run a rental property in the area (this will generally include council tax and additional local fees), pricing history, home values, rental activity and annual trends, buying rates, rental rates, turnover rates, employment rates, and average household income. Also keep your eye on convenience. Find out if the area includes easy and enticing shopping areas, parks, schools, and public transportation.

Chapter 4:
Target Properties

Well done getting through the section on targeting locations. There's one more thing you need to know about to get you down the track as fast as possible: targeting properties.

So, you've found a suitable location to work in, but now you need to look around for properties you can take over and sublet. I'll explain where to look for available properties in your selected area and a list of criteria you should routinely check for each prospective property and as part of your process.

You'll get a list of all the characteristics of a property that could make a very nice HMO. And again, even if your property model is not an HMO, I'll explain the main things you should look for in any worthwhile rent-to-rent property type.

Maybe you can't tell because you're moving so fast, but you're already ahead of much of the competition. Keep your foot steady on the accelerator and your eyes upon the road ahead of you.

22. Where do I look to find available properties and opportunities?

Once you've narrowed your target location, it's time to search for properties that suit your business plan. Looking online for a property is fast and easy. You can find available properties on sites like Zoopla, Rightmove, Home.co.uk, and OnTheMarket. You can even search local networking sites for rental opportunities. However, online is not the only place to look. Because so much of the world's commerce is now conducted online, it can be easy to forget that going out into the real world can generate some of your best opportunities. Go to the area you're interested in and drive or walk around in search of property for rent. While you're in the area, pick up a stack of local papers and estate booklets/flyers for available properties. Meet and greet with other local estate agents from the area, agents, landlords, property owners, and investors.

23. What is a client avatar and why do I need one?

A client avatar is one of the most important tools I use when going into a new location or selecting a new property to sublet. It's a profile of your customer; I make one for the customer profile I'm realistically serving, and the ideal customer profile I want; sometimes these aren't always the same and seeing the difference can make the difference.

A client avatar is similar to the customer analysis in your business plan, but this is more in-depth. I used to think the customer analysis was enough, but having a profile of the client base you have, or that you're aiming for, is so effective. It's like a mini-SWOT analysis of your prospective customer, and by compiling these general demographics, you can make a property more profitable, an agreement more attractive, and a marketing campaign focused and effective.

If this is your business start-up phase, or if you're still in your early years of growth, your businesses will benefit most from this exercise. Analysing your customer-base in this way allows you to speak in a more compelling, meaningful, emotional, and lasting way. You may reach fewer overall people when you put the marketing out there, but the people you do reach will be a much better compatibility to your ideal client, and for your property. The quality and calibre of the lead of prospect will be far superior than a wide-spread campaign in most cases.

Creating a client avatar also helps you understand your product and service better. By understanding better who your target tenant is, you have a better idea of what conveniences and luxuries the individual will be interested in. You'll be able to know which features will likely mean the most to the individual. You can market better and provide more value.

24. How do I select a good property for HMO?

On the back of the previous question about where to find available properties, is how to find them. There are three basic tactics I use to select a suitable property in which to invest. Dig through local listings, market your business to the area, and network in the area. Searching through listings of available properties in the area seems obvious. It's the last two tactics that are often overlooked, skipped, and therefore could cost you some of the best opportunities you'll find. Not to mention, if you market your business to the local area, and you make a habit of engaging with other local professionals, you're building a long-term rapport with the community which will surely benefit you in the years of business to come.

In terms of marketing your rent-to-rent management business, consider direct mail marketing to related businesses and property owners. Customise the marketing to fit the proper audience. Consider running Google Ads or Facebook Ads for your business and set those ads to target your primary location(s). Look for landlord listings online and send them a letter directly, or email them your offer to manage properties with a guaranteed rent agreement. The more people exposed to your business, the more business you acquire.

Network in real life and online. Use your business LinkedIn profile to connect with interested parties. LinkedIn is the Facebook of the professional world. Network the hell out of it. Facebook is also abundant with groups you can join for networking in the industry, in the exact locations you're targeting. Don't stop your network at estate agents and property management professionals. Build a rapport with local cleaning services and repairman or contractors. Remember to network in real life, too. Find related networking events in your target area(s) and attend them. Go prepared with your business card and perhaps a one-page piece of marketing to quickly illustrate your amazing offer.

25. What makes a good property for an HMO?

If you're in search of a property to sublet as an HMO, the first point to keep in mind is what it will take to let that property as an HMO. You likely need to stay within a budget, sometimes a very small budget, so you want a property that will require the least amount of renovations or updates. The exception to this is if you have money to invest in updating and renovating. A healthy profit can be made in either situation, but keep in mind that typically the newer the accommodations, the higher the rent. For this reason, it's crucial that you do a thorough investigation of the local health and safety codes for your location and then compare that to the property you have in mind. If the property is going to need costly upgrades, calculate for this when you make your final decision.

Another point that holds weight in your search for the perfect HMO property is the tenants. If you've done your due diligence, you should have a fairly good idea of the demand for rentals in your area. You may even have an idea of whether tenants in your area are families, singles, students, professionals, and you may be able to determine the average age and income of these prospects as well. Look for a property that will be enticing to your target audience and easy to fill, not just once, but over the course of time as rental agreements expire.

With regard to tenancy, another key factor to consider is whether the property is already occupied with tenants. In some cases, this can be great news, but not always. If the unit has tenants that are planning to continue occupying the unit, this can take a simple step out of the equation and save you from looking for new tenants. However, this can turn into a somewhat sticky situation if you intend to raise rental costs, make changes to the property, or invite more tenants into the property. You'll have to work gently around the existing tenant(s) or remove them. If you're showing the property to prospective tenants while current tenants are still occupying the space, again, operate gently and with convenience toward them. Upsetting the cordial balance can risk a successful showing and tenants with animosity (even if it's unjustified) can sabotage your viewings. Consider what expenses you'll be looking at in order to successfully fill the property with tenants.

Look for a property that will be easy to maintain. You'll want a property that has been more or less well-cared-for historically so you aren't acquiring a list of serious property issues hidden just below the surface. Certainly, don't skip steps here; check the plumbing, the heating and the electricals. Check doors, windows, and additional security measures. Check the roof and elsewhere for signs of damp. The easier the property is to maintain, the lower the expense for you.

Once you've found a few properties that are worthy of your investment, talk to the property owners. Find out what kind of deals they're willing to make on the rental costs and on the management of the building. Talking to the property owner will also give you great insight into previous tenants which can serve you going forward in your hunt for new tenants. Ask the property owners about the terms and conditions of the mortgages or insurance policies they hold, and whether subletting is in violation.

Each of these key factors, combined with the local estate agent's economy data you've gathered, should give you more than enough confidence to select the right property. Remember to take your time in these steps upfront and it will save you trouble in the future. Once your rent-to-rent business is underway, you'll find ways to speed up this process, but for now, work slowly and diligently, and pick up the pace down the road.

26. What makes a good property for other models?

Essentially, you're still looking for the same key factors in a single-family rental, or lodging, that you would in an HMO opportunity. Ultimately, the idea is to look for a property that will meet your rental needs, and it won't take a large investment to get it there. Because single-family properties are somewhat less stringent on regulations, they can sometimes be a less costly investment as they won't need so much updating to be compliant. You'll still need to pay attention to tenancy, property maintenance, and of course, the guaranteed rent you agree on with the property owner.

Chapter 5:
Negotiate and Sign with Property Owners

Now you're approaching the back half of the track and it's time to scream down the line like lightning. Understanding how the negotiation process should work with a property owner is going to make the whole interaction more seamless and smoother.

It can be intimidating to get to the point of negotiations and not quite know what to do next. For you, there is no intimidation because you know with the lessons in this next section you'll be prepared to work with property owners, make them an enticing offer, draw up the contracts, and include all the important details.

We'll start with exactly how to approach an owner about their available property in the first place. I'll teach you what to say and how to say it. You'll learn which insightful questions to ask, and how to ease the concerns of a nervous property owner.

When negotiating with your property owner, there are several key factors to work out: is the property permitted to operate as an HMO? Who pays for any necessary upgrades and renovations? What's the best practice when it comes to paying for utilities on the property?

This section will explain all the crucial pieces that should come from your negotiation and should be documented in your agreement. Finally, we'll take a look at closing the deal or walking away, and the benefit you might not expect.

Stay strapped in as we pick up speed and answer questions about the negotiation process with property owners.

27.   How do I approach a property owner about an HMO opportunity?

One of my favourite techniques for approaching a property owner is by getting *them* to approach *you* with interest and curiosity about your offer. This will only happen, however, if they've been exposed to your business. How? Marketing. Gain exposure in your selected area with effective marketing and networking.

We'll go into more detail about your marketing plan as we go along, but briefly, there are several marketing techniques that tend to work simply and effectively when I introduce my business to a new area. Direct mail marketing is inexpensive and effective if you do it right. Don't just send a flyer with your name and what you do. Put your service into context for your audience and deliver a relevant "prize" of some kind. Include a call to action – that call to action can be enticing the property owner to approach you.

Another effective technique for approaching property owners is to place yourself in a pool of them and network the hell out of it. Visit a few local seminars or events in your selected area to meet new prospects and professionals.

If an even more direct route is your style, try walking into local real estate and agency offices and introducing yourself with a few business cards. Email or call property owners to let them know you're interested in managing an available property they have.

Once you've made contact, in many ways it just gets easier from there. Be honest and transparent about how you'd like to work together. Ask insightful questions and build a rapport. You don't need to make your hard offer right away. When you've built a rapport, consider the prospect and follow up in a couple of days if it looks good and checks out. Then is the time to make an offer.

28. What should I say and do when negotiating with a property owner?

Be honest and clear about your vision for the property and how you'd like it to operate. Your property owner may or may not be familiar with how subletting works and why it's a benefit to them, so take the time to explain how you'd like to manage the property and its tenants. As you negotiate, there are five main points to cover.

Discuss with your property owner whether small changes and renovations can be made to the property to update and comply with codes and regulations. Decide who will be responsible for the cost of those renovations, but be prepared for it to be you. This is an especially sweet part to your offer in many cases.

Find out whether your property model plan is in violation of any terms or conditions set forth by either the mortgage lender or the insurance company. If so, discuss legitimate ways to resolve this concern or work with it to still generate a healthy and profitable rental property.

Explain what kind of tenancy you'd like to fill. Describe the number of residents you'd like to accommodate, for approximately how long, and pinpoint the primary candidate type you'd like to attract to the property.

Make your offer for a guaranteed rental price. Explain that while the price you pay may be a bit lower than the market asking price, the rent is guaranteed even if a resident fails to pay or when the unit is vacant.
Decide who will manage the property and pay for the maintenance and upkeep. In most cases, this will be you. It's an enticing factor in your offer and takes a great burden from the property owner.

Negotiating with your property owner is much the same as negotiating in any field or industry at the heart of it. You want your prospect to feel safe with you and trust you. You want your prospect to find value in your offer. And, you want to give your prospect a call to action. At this point in your negotiation, it's appropriate to present a written agreement for the property owner to review and consider. Ultimately, to sign, but not necessarily on the spot. It's normal and healthy for you both to take a couple of days to consider the agreement. But don't wait too long; the agreement loses its sense of urgency. Keep the screws gently to your prospect by following up in a day or so to see what it takes to get them to sign with you.

29. How do I answer questions and ease concerns?

Answer questions and ease concerns by offering open and transparent conversation. Instil more confidence and comfort to your prospect by providing examples of previous success. This can be your own successful rent-to-rent investments, or you can use the case studies of others who've been successful with the same "game-plan" you implement. The latter is especially helpful if you're just starting out and don't have other rent-to-rent properties under your management to showcase.

Another way to ease concerns answer questions from property owners, lenders, or investors, is to provide a clear and formal account of your business plan. This helps your audience understand the value you provide, the financial plans and records for the business, who your target clients are, your top competitors, your experience, and your annual goals. Being transparent with these details, at least to an extent, can calm anxious investors, lenders, or partners.

The key is to be clear and honest. You shouldn't need to conduct shady business, and it's a fair bet that if you do, it will return to haunt you.

30. How can I make sure an HMO is permitted at the property?

First, ask and verify. The property owner should know or can check with the proper channels to confirm operating as an

HMO is permitted on the property. Two main entities are usually the final say in whether or not an HMO rental is allowed: the mortgage lender and the insurance provider. If there's no mortgage on the property and it's owned outright - bonus - you don't have to worry about the terms and conditions of the mortgage lender. You must still verify an HMO rental will be permitted by the insurance provider. It wouldn't hurt for you to know of several insurance providers that do not prevent an HMO operation, in case your property owner considers switching in order to move ahead with your plan.

Last, get it in writing and put it in writing. It's not uncommon to ask the property owner for some form of documentation that indicates an HMO operation is permitted on the property. It's also a smart idea to make reference to this point in the contract you present to your prospect. Make your agreement specify that the property owner is responsible for the verification of the terms and conditions of both the mortgage lender and the insurance company to ensure the operation of an HMO is not a violation.

31.   Who pays for renovations and upgrades?

You pay for renovations and upgrades; it's almost always you. This is a large draw to your offer. In some cases, the property owner may want to pay for or manage renovations. This takes a significant strain off of your investment budget, but make sure to stay on top of these changes to make sure they are made expeditiously, especially if you're not the one paying for or managing the work.

32.   Who pays for utilities at the property?

Who pays for the utilities on the property can go three different ways. Your property owner could hold all utilities in his or her name, include it in the price they charge you for guaranteed rent, and thus you would include it in your sublet cost.

You could put utilities in the name(s) of your tenant(s). In this case, you'll have the extra hassle of continuously switching utilities between you and your tenants that come and go. You also risk your other tenants suffering the loss of a utility if one tenant is negligent with the payment.

The best practice, I find, is to put the utilities in the name of the property manager - you. You'll be responsible for paying utilities on the property in addition to guaranteed rent, but you can easily include this cost in the general rental rate of the property. There's no risk for utilities being shut off and there's no hassle in switching names back and forth as tenants move in and out. Plus, advertising your accommodation with all utilities included often creates an enticing draw to prospective tenants.

33.   How can I get out of the contract early, if I'm unable to find tenants?

There may be an unforeseen circumstance that creates the need to leave your contract early. For example, a local contamination makes the property unrentable until the local vicinity can be cleared and considered safe again. It is possible to get out of the agreement you make with your landlord early, but it must be done fairly and in accordance with the law. When you create an agreement between you and the property owner, make sure this is some type of fixed-term tenancy agreement; typically, an assured shorthold tenancy. It is within any type of fixed-term agreement that a break clause can be implemented. A break clause is a term within your agreement that allows either you or the landlord to end the tenancy before the end of the agreed upon fixed-term. A break clause should take extra care to specify exactly how, when, and where a notice of breaking the contract should be delivered. The notice should take extra care to use the proper language set forth in the agreement in order to maintain the validity of the notice.

The break clause in your agreement should specify exactly who can break the tenancy; in most cases it's either the tenant or the landlord, in order to maintain fairness between the trader and the consumer. Even if you include in your contract largely unfair conditions the other person agrees to, the law still protects them from exploitation and will nullify the agreement made.

Unlike evictions and other notices, there is no formal requirement for the amount of time between notice and action in the case of a break clause. If you both agree that a notice served will take full effect within 24 hours, that's valid; so long as you both agree to it, and you both can implement it.

34.   How do I close the deal with property owners?

When the time comes, put your offer on the table - but don't leave it there. Set the expectation, graciously, that you intend to make an investment in managing a property soon and you'd like it to be this one, but the offer expires eventually. Put a specific or approximate date of expiry on the table to increase the sense of urgency for the prospect. Make the offer you want. Compromise if necessary. Don't get hung up on trying to land one fish when the ocean is full. There are other properties out there for you. If it's too difficult to persuade your prospect to sign, move on. They aren't ready and you might find them to be a difficult customer in the long run.

Chapter 6:

Negotiate and Sign with Tenants

At this point, you've learned the basics of rent-to-rent business. The knowledge of contract types and how to use them is now under your belt. You know exactly how to target a location and search for potential properties within that area.

You've found a property, found the owner, struck negotiations, and closed the deal. A property is now yours to convert to an HMO and manage effectively. It's time to run your next two steps parallel to one another. As you begin your process of updates and renovations for your HMO unit, it's a smart idea to start feeling around for prospective tenants and marketing the space to a local audience.

This is where you really pick up speed in the race.

In this section, you'll learn where to look for tenants and how to entice them. We will break down the traits and characteristics that make a good tenant, and how you can find and determine these qualities in your applicants.

You'll learn how to manage the viewing process in a professional and unbiased manner, tricks and techniques for improving the viewing process, and how to collect helpful observations.

I'll explain which factors to consider when deciding what you'll charge for rent, and how to generate the appropriate contractual agreement for your tenant(s).

Keep your grip on the wheel at 10 and 2 and focus on that finish line. Here we go!

35.   How do I find tenants?

The good news is since you did your homework on the area before selecting it, you probably have a relatively good idea of the need for apartments in your area. Now you just need to get yourself (or your offer) in front of your target audience. This step is about marketing. Take excellent pictures of the residence, inside and out. Pictures are truly worth a thousand words in this case and it's usually the first thing that draws interest to the unit. Write a descriptive and compelling ad that highlights all the excellent features of the property. Make sure to present a clear and obvious way for others to get in touch with you. Run your ad on Craigslist and other local networking sites. Put it on Zoopla and similar sites that prospective tenants regularly check for rental availability. Put it in the local paper. Seek out places you know your target audience will visit and put ads there. For example, if you're trying to attract young professionals and students, make your offer visible on campus bulletin boards, cafe workspaces, or run target campaigns on Facebook. Market the property quickly and clearly and the tenants will come to find you.

36.   What makes a good tenant for an HMO?

Whether or not a tenant is a good match for you can largely be determined by three sources: the pre-screening process, the viewing, and the screening process. However, you need an idea of what you're looking for in a tenant, in order to determine whether the trait is there. You want to know you're subletting to a responsible and respectful individual who will treat the property with the same responsibility and respect. A good tenant shows signs of good credit and stable income. A good tenant will have a clean criminal background check and rental history. It's preferable if you can find a tenant with a history of residing in previous residences for consistent intervals of time. If you see a pattern of tenancy that lasts a year, two, maybe more, then chances are the pattern will continue with you. If a tenancy shows a history of skipping and jumping around, it's not necessarily bad, but it's probably not a perfect fit for your HMO. These kinds of tenants might be a better match for a lodging situation.

These details will help you determine if your prospective tenants are a good match for you economically, but there's a vital set of characteristics that will set some prospective tenants apart from others: honesty, respect, and cleanliness. It's definitely not asking too much to find a tenant that demonstrates these key traits. It goes beyond trusting that your tenant will treat the property with respect and be honest with you. A tenant with these traits will take a sense of pride and care in the property as if it were their own. If something gets broken, they will tell you. If they run into financial hardship, they will be honest with you and not take advantage of you or the property. There's a sense of personal investment and ownership all their own that leaves a property manager feeling confident and secure.

37.   What is the viewing process and how should it go?

The viewing process generally happens at the same time as, or just after, the pre-screening process, and just before the screening process. To understand the viewing process, let's briefly examine all three processes.

The pre-screening process generally follows any marketing you've just put out to find tenants for your property. Pre-screening can happen over the phone or email, or it can happen in person as part of the viewing process. In the pre-screening process, you're asking general questions to get a feel for the individual. Though the pre-screening process has a casual and comfortable feeling about it, treat it as a business process. Ask each tenant the same general pre-screening questions in order to avoid any chance of your questions having any sort of discriminatory edge. In the pre-screening process, you would typically ask general questions like:

- Where are you from?
- What do you do for fun?
- What do you do for work?
- Why are you moving?
- What's the earliest you can move in?
- What's your average monthly income?
- Will anyone be moving with you?
- Do you have pets?
- Do you smoke?
- Will you consent to a credit and background check?
- Will you be able to provide references?
- Do you have sufficient funds for a deposit?

The viewing process is when you show the prospective tenant through the entire property. If you haven't done a pre-screening process yet, it's a good time to do it as you walk the property together with the tenant. It helps to break the ice and make for easy conversation.

There are a few rules to remember when conducting the viewing process. Again, ask every prospect the same set of questions to avoid any misconstrued discrimination. Show the entire space. Any area the tenant is allowed to go within the property is where you should show them. Even basement and attic space (if applicable) should be viewed. Include any major appliances that come as part of the unit. If the prospect is interested, give them an application to fill out and ask if they will consent to a credit and background check. Additionally, if you're part of a redress scheme, you may be supplied with a pamphlet to give to each of your applicants which covers renter's rights and so forth. Do not make a hasty decision on the spot to sublet to someone. Perhaps the most important step comes next.

After the viewing process, and usually within the next couple of days, you conduct a screening process for each of the tenant applicants. During this step, you'll check into references, background checks, and rental history to determine whether the tenant will be a good economical fit. Now you have all the information you need to select the best tenants for your property.

38.　What is staging and should I do it?

Staging is the act of setting up a vacant space to look homey and liveable. It's used quite often in the buying and selling of homes, but it has caught on quite well for rental viewings, as well. Staging usually consists of placing some of the more traditional pieces of furniture into each room in hopes of conveying the room's potential. This is usually furniture like dining tables and chairs, a couch and living room seating, and beds. If the property already has tenants in it that you're working around, you can't really set staging, but hopefully the current tenant's furniture will serve the same purpose more or less.

Staging is similar to, but not the same as providing a furnished property. In many cases, before the new tenant moves in, the staging furniture will be removed to make way for the tenant's own furnishings. In the case of a furnished unit, you provide the major furnishings and leave them in the property to be used by your tenants as part of the entire package.

As to whether or not you should stage your property for the viewing process, it's mostly a matter of preference. In all likelihood, whether you stage or not isn't going to make or break the deal, but it can help prospects to have a vision for the room with a few key pieces in place.

Keep in mind that staging will likely require you to purchase the furniture you'll use, unless you're able to acquire decent second-hand furniture. Purchasing furniture for staging can influence your budget. Removing the furniture when it's time for your tenant(s) to arrive can also cost you time and money.

39.   What do I charge for rent?

What you charge is mostly up to you, but you want to give a figure based on information, and not just an arbitrary number. The first helpful rule is that rent is to closely examine rental rates for similar properties in the area. Of course, if you are renting out each room separately, check out sites like Spare Room to get an idea. Remember if you make upgrades and improvements to the property before subletting, you have increased the value of the home.

If you'll be keeping utilities in your name and making that part of your attractive offer, you can increase rent costs to reasonably cover these expenses. To be fair, add the average cost of all the property's utilities and divide that by the number of tenants you'll have. This way, each tenant pays approximately the same for utilities. You may be able to increase the rental cost or tack on additional costs for inclusions like off-street parking, furnishings, pets, or even convenient location. Use these guides and the local pricing to determine a fair and reasonable rental cost which will still make the income you need to support the property and make a profit.

40.   How do I close the deal with tenants?

Closing with a tenant, in my opinion, starts at the beginning of the process; marketing the unit. This is the first impression of the property my prospective tenants will see; I want to do everything within my power to make that first impression enticing. I want the prospect to want this sublet before they apply or even come to view it in person.

To make the first impressions as compelling as possible, I provide clear, well-lit pictures of all the spaces that come as part of the property, including parking and outdoor spaces. I include ample pictures of the private room being rented and any special accommodations that come with the room, such as additional storage space or room size, additional widows, or attached bathrooms or balconies. I make sure to list all the additional accommodations included with the sublet, such as utilities included in the rental cost, free internet Wi-Fi and kitchen appliances.

When I pre-screen, I use this as another time to work the close indirectly. This is an opportunity to build a rapport with the prospective tenant, but more than that, it's a way for you to filter tenants that will work for you or not (without being discriminatory). The pre-screening is a chance for me to describe the kind of living environment, location, neighbourhood, and expectations that the tenant can expect with your property. This is another opportunity for you to demonstrate how desirable your property is.

Viewing the property with the prospective tenant is a great time to hook them on the features and benefits of the property. This is your face-to-face chance to market your property. That's more or less your sales pitch to the tenant.

After the viewing, the prospective tenant should submit an application for the sublet of the property, and with that, you conduct a series of checks on the prospect. If everything checks out and you like the tenant, you will invite them to review your contract. You can do this in person, or via phone and email, but the key is to not sit on it too long. As soon as you give contract paperwork to the prospective tenant, start a countdown on the expiry of the offer before you have to move on to the next prospective tenant.

I usually give my prospective tenant a call, and let them know I'd love to have them as a tenant. I send an email of the contract and ask them to review it and let me know about any questions. I put a 2-business day countdown on that and if I haven't heard back from the prospect by then, I let them know I'm extending offers to other interested parties and working on a first-come-first-serve basis. This usually sets a sense of urgency and the property is filled within a week.

If your prospective tenant wants to negotiate the terms and costs of the sublet, that's up to you. You can adjust your contract if you want to, but you're not obligated to negotiate. If you don't want to budge on price, terms, or conditions, you don't have to. It's ok to move onto the next prospective tenant. It helps to have a couple of backup selections in case your first picks are no longer available to move in.

Chapter 7:
Manage a Small HMO Renovation

Now we slam into overdrive as you take on the most challenging stretch of the track: how to manage a small renovation in order to prepare a property to run legitimately as an HMO.

There's a lot to keep in mind as you take on this project, but the lessons in this section are here to help you. Next, we'll take a look at exactly what it takes to manage a renovation and what you can expect.

Even if cases other than an HMO, it may be required that you perform some updates on the property to comply with health and safety regulations. If you're making an HMO from an AST, almost certainly there will be renovations to make, as the regulations are even more stringent in the case of a house of multiple occupants.

In this section, you'll learn about the legal requirements for an HMO operation, including the various requirements of the council for health, safety, and acceptable living conditions. There are space requirements, documentation requirements, electrical; gas; and fire safety requirements. You'll even need to compare your list of necessary changes and updates to the list of changes for which the government requires you have authorized planning permission or building approval.

Here we go; heading for the home stretch.

41.   How do I update an existing HMO property to meet standards and regulations?

If you intend to have multiple people in one property, as separate households, the biggest update you need to make sure you've completed is acquiring a licence for such a unit.

Although the property may already have a licence to function as HMO, licences expire after five years and you must renew before it expires or you will be in violation of having multiple occupancies without proper licencing. This can result in as little as a fine, or as much as the revocation of your right to function an HMO property.

In most cases, if there are five or more individuals living in a property, as more than one household, a licence is required. In some cases, as few as three individuals totalling more than one household constitutes an HMO property. It may depend on how many storeys the property is, as well.

To find out about the specific licencing requirements for properties in your area, search the government database by postcode to confirm what defines an HMO and what kind of licencing is needed. In most cases, an HMO is defined by having five or more occupants totalling more than one household and sharing bathroom and kitchen facilities.

The second most important update is meeting and adhering to the required conditions of a property to function as an HMO.

When you check for and apply for licencing in your area, the council will specify all of the conditions which must be met for a property to function as an HMO.

Be prepared for the property to allow for a certain square-footage of space per person. This will depend on the size of the property, the number of occupants, the shared and/or private facilities, and the location. The Local Authority will also require as a condition that the property manager has no criminal record or practice of any breach in law or code.

Annually, it will be your responsibility to submit records to the council that demonstrate your adherence to all laws, regulations, and inspections for your HMO. This will almost always include certificates of safety and/or inspection for gas, electricity, fire and emergency, security, and major appliances.

Depending on your specific location, property, and occupants, the council may request additional updates to your property to meet the standards for a proper HMO in your area. The Local Authority will inform you of any additional requirements for your particular case during the filing process and a reasonable amount of time is generally given for you to meet these additional requirements.

42. How do I manage a small renovation to create an HMO property?

If you're the one paying for the renovations then you're likely the one managing it. You've probably got a list of all kinds of expenses and steps that need to happen before you can market the property. Organise your list into top priorities, tasks that need to happen soon, and nice-to-haves. Start with the changes that you absolutely cannot live without. This is usually anything to satisfy the requirements of the health and safety regulations in your local area.

From the projects you absolutely cannot live without, which can you afford to start right now, and which are the tasks that will take the longest. Assuming you'll be able to afford at least all the work to satisfy health and safety regulations, you want to begin with the projects that will take the longest in most situations. There may be a factor that overrides this, but typically, to make the project roll along at an efficient pace, you want to have the longer projects running in the background while you deal with the short-term tasks in the forefront.

When you're closing in on the completion of projects that were essential, you can review your budget and determine next the goals that need to be done soon and the nice to haves. Which on these lists will increase the value of the property by implementing it? If it's an affordable option, take on those tasks next. If your budget is getting low, consider which tasks you have left that will take little to no financial commitment and work on those as much as you're able.

It may be the case that you'll have to schedule your renovations in a Part One and Part Two, and that's completely okay. In fact, it's often a safer idea, because you can spread out the cost of renovations and allow some relief from income in the interim. It takes considerable stress off your year-one budget.

43. What are the legal requirements for an HMO?

If you're operating an HMO, there are a few legal steps you do not want to skip. Doing so runs you the risk of fines, cessation of your operation, legal issues, and even imprisonment.

Definitely register your business with the council. If you're operating an HMO, you need to select a business structure and register it. You can only skip this step if you're subletting an AST or a lodging accommodation.

Register your HMO property with the council. In the same way, you need to register your business for your HMO operation to adhere to the law, you need to register the property as an HMO, too. If you manage more than one HMO, each needs to be registered. As a registered business and HMO, there will be several forms of documentation you'll be responsible to submit on a regular basis, such as annually updated gas safety certificates for each of your HMO properties and safety certificates for all major appliances.

Definitely join a redress scheme. If you fail to join an authorised redress scheme, you can be fined up to £5,000 and have your licence revoked.

Don't forget to pay the council tax. Failure to do so quickly will revoke the opportunity to make the payment in instalments. Failing to pay it all together results in the seizure of personal property and goods until enough value is confiscated to pay for the council tax.

Do not violate the terms and agreements set forth in either the mortgage contract or the insurance policy for the property. Some mortgages and insurance policies include stipulations about rentals and occupancy. Though the mortgage and the insurance policy may be in the name of the property owner, it's still you - the one who takes the sublet action - who will be responsible for this neglect.

Don't sublet without the owner's consent. One of the biggest ethical concerns with subletting is deception. Be transparent with property owners about what you want to do.

Definitely do not rent to illegal immigrants. Do not sublet to individuals that do not have legal permission to enter or live in the UK. A scenario like this is tempting to the corrupt rent-to-rent business owner because the cost of rent can be jacked up to take advantage of desperate people who need housing. Illegal immigrants can do little in the way to protect themselves against these shady landlords and rental agreements because there is no legal recourse for them.

Trustworthy business professionals will always officially check a tenant's right to rent. If you cannot prove that you've taken this step and documented your investigation, you'll almost certainly be fined. For any tenancy starting on or after 2014 (or 2016 in some areas), you'll need to perform this check before finalising your contract and move-in date with your tenants. To investigate this and document your investigation, the housing authorities require that you ask your prospective tenant for original, genuine, documentation and that you save copies of that documentation at least 28 days before the tenancy begins. There are some cases in which you do not need to check, such as providing social housing or accommodations to refugees, but you'll always want to make sure you've got this base covered.

44.   What are the spatial requirements for an HMO?

If you're operating an HMO property, there are requirements for how much space a human needs to fulfil health and safety regulations. In an HMO, each sleeping room must allow for so much space per person.

- 6.51 m2 for one person over 10 years of age
- 10.22 m2 for two persons over 10 years
- No more than two persons sleeping in a room
- No shared space can be a sleeping space
- No room smaller than 4.64 m2 is allowed to be a sleeping room
- No part of a room should be a ceiling height of less than 1.5m
- Every sleeping space must include natural light and ventilation.

Additionally, you'll find regulations such as:

- For every four tenants in a property, one bathroom is required

For every five tenants:
- The shared kitchen space must be at least 7 m2 and at least 1.8 m wide
- An additional room for living space must be included and must be no smaller than 11 m2

For six to ten tenants:
- The kitchen must be at least 10 m2 and at least 1.8 m wide
- The den or living space must be at least 16.5 m2

In addition, an HMO property should adhere to the following in order for the property to be deemed safe for living:
- The property must not be in general neglect
- The building must be stable
- The building must be free from excessive damp
- The property should be designed with a safe layout
- Each sleeping room or main living space should provide ample natural light
- Each room should include proper ventilation
- The property should provide working hot and cold water from faucets and showers
- The property must maintain proper drainage, waste water, and sanitation
- The property must provide a safe environment for cooking food

The Local Authority is known to inspect properties to ensure they are safe, well-managed, and not overpopulated. If your property is inspected and found to be in violation of any of these requirements, you could be subject to a financial penalty of up to £30,000 as an alternative to prosecution. It's not worth getting caught; do it right.

45. How should I lay out a small HMO refurb?

To answer this question most effectively, let's assume for the sake of example that you've entered into an agreement with a landlord for a small renovation to turn an AST private rental into a registered HMO with 3 bedrooms. Currently, the property has two bedrooms on the upper level and on the lower level, there's a spare den that you're converting to a bedroom. Whichever room you convert to an additional bedroom, it should be a side room off of the shared common spaces and not amongst them. Keep in mind that conversion will need to meet its own standards and regulations regarding size, light, windows and doors, locks, and safety and electrical. It's common to transform an additional spare bedroom, den, study, or dining room, so long as you leave a properly-sized shared living-room space, kitchen, and bathroom(s). Shared common spaces cannot double as a resident's personal living space.

Let's assume now that you've made the renovation for a third bedroom downstairs, so now you can fit three tenants into your HMO. Assess the flow of traffic into, through, and out of the house. Is one entry busier than another? Consider as part of your renovation that a small, covered porch, or entry on the outside of the property to make a convenient entrance from the very start. This helps to block tenants and visitors from the elements as they unlock the door, or rearrange items being carried inside. Each tenant will have their own set of keys so start with convenience right there and assign a coloured key to each tenant; red-yellow-blue (we'll say), and that colour is theirs, throughout the property. Once inside, consider creating or updating an entryway. This is an especially simple and small renovation that makes an enormous difference in rental value and mitigating wear and tear on the common spaces of the property. Make your entryway large enough to accommodate the needs of three individual residents and general guest and visitor entry.

Include closet and storage space enough so that three individuals each have their own. This can be done quite easily with a bench-storage entry design. In the entries I update, I include a bench unit that can be a seat for putting on your shoes. The bench opens and inside are three units, one for each colour. This is entry storage for boots and shoes. Higher up the wall above the bench, a locker-space style storage cupboard is installed on the wall. This is where my tenants usually store keys, glasses, hats, gloves, and the general items you drop or take as one enters or leaves the home. I include a closet that can hold and hide other items, mostly coats and shoes. In the closet is a set of coloured cubbie blocks that will hold a pair of shoes in each cubbie, nine cubbies for each tenant, colour-coded. Each tenant receives 10 colour-coded hangers for their coats. There's also a thin railing table in the entry to temporarily place items down, store keys, change, and mail, and charge cell phones. There's also a coat hook on the wall for visitors and guests. By adding an entryway, you save your tenants trodding through the common areas and into the bedrooms with heavy outdoor boots and shoes, and messes. continue to use colour-coding (or numbers; 1, 2, 3...) around the shared common spaces where necessary; the kitchen and the bathroom in particular. In both the kitchen and bathroom areas, each tenant should be given equal storage space for personal belongings. Closets, drawers, and cabinets should be equal and designated via your colour-coding system.

In your common spaces, it can actually work out to your advantage to supply the shared furnishings, from appliances to furniture. These are often items that provide tax breaks for your business, and it saves the hassle of squabbles among tenants who share their own furniture in the shared spaces. In the shared living areas, make sure there's enough seating for at least each tenant; guests too if manageable.

In the kitchen area, depending on how detailed you want to get and how much you intend to furnish, you can even assign each tenant their own basic, colour-coded set of plates, dishes, cups, cookware, and cutlery. In the bathroom, you might even provide each tenant with linens and towels to match their colour. I even provide equal refrigerator space in an equal and convenient way; one mini-fridge for each tenant. The space was such that three small units could be fit under a counter space, with a drawer about it, and a coordinating cupboard space above the counter. It doesn't mean they can't use their own things in any of these scenarios, it just means you provided the same accommodations to all tenants which will achieve a rental of a higher value. Having equal but designated space and furnishings, it stops disagreements before they can ever start.

When it comes down to each bedroom, the doors should include a locking mechanism, but it's advised that the mechanism allow for turn-lock handles, which provide a swift escape from a room without a key in the case of fire or other emergencies. This is more than just advisement, really; it's a fire and emergency safety regulation. Inside, provide each tenant with the same items, and quality of items, suitable for a bedroom. You don't need to colour-code doors or decorate rooms in designated colours only; people will know which room of three is there's. Again, depending on how detailed you want to get and how much you'll be furnishing. It's my personal preference to supply All common space furnishings and require tenants to furnish their rooms themselves; which I find is usually preferable because my tenants will want to use their own beds and desks etc. If you're operating a vacation-style or accommodation-style property, you'll likely provide bedroom furnishings yourself, just as a hotel or an AirBnB would.

Try to provide about as equal a set of major accommodations as possible. Try to have roughly the same size rooms, with the same number of windows and roughly the same closet space. This isn't always exactly possible, so as long as all rooms meet health and safety regulations, you can rent the ones with more space, more windows, attached bathrooms, for a bit more money than the room without these features.

46.   What additional conveniences and accommodations should I consider for an HMO?

Conveniences you want to provide outside of what is required by law is basically up to you (and your property owner), but the more convenient the property, the more you can charge for rent. Consider installing laundry services inside the property that can be shared between tenants. Provide equal secure storage to all tenants in a basement, attic, or other storage space. When making renovations and updates, consider the number of tenants you'll be accommodating and then account for that in your installation.

In the spaces I've rented out, I like to be the one who pays utilities on the property, and I build that cost into the total price of the rented room. So heat, water, electric and trash removal are all my responsibility, but I am financially compensated for providing it. Beyond that, I also provide free internet and television access with a house subscription to various streaming services. In one HMO property, I sublet to four young lads, so as part of the welcome, I gifted them a Playstation4. They've all extended their tenancy multiple times.

In some locations I've worked, the property makes more sense to sublet furnished. Don't think of this as an added expense, but rather, a way for you to wow your tenant for a small investment in furniture. It can pay off in the same way; retaining your residents year over year. If you furnish the bedroom spaces, provide a mattress, boxspring, and frame, two sets of bedsheets and pillowcases, two pillows, a comforter, a blanket, and a small area rug on the floor. Include a wardrobe, chest, or bureau, a closet, a bookshelf, a desk, chair, and bedside table. I even include small bonuses like a new trash can, lamp, desk set, and curtains which are neutral, but also easily removed and replaced or left off at the tenant's preference.

Don't just think about today; think about tomorrow. How will people be living in the next decade? Consider how the added feature of green products and appliances will increase the value of the property. Solar panels that support renewable energy can have an attractive appeal on the market.

Homes need to not only suit the changing ethical and environmental climate, but the technological one. Homes and residences need to be equipped to be readily compatible with technologies that run the person and the home. This can be something as simple as including USB charging outlets in the home where electrical sockets and plugs used to be the only method.

If you're able, consider going for a property that will allow the tenant some freedom in a small outside area like a backyard, patio, porch, or balcony. When tenants have the prospect of a rental space that will allow them some freedom in making the outdoor space a little more of their own, it becomes a top-dollar commodity. But keep it in perspective! If you invest in a property with a large landscape, beautiful gardens, and a crystal clear pool, you will need to pay to maintain these. Don't go overboard. See if you can find something that gives your tenants a piece of outdoor solace all their own, but not something that requires a personal gardener on site.

Go out of your way to provide other conveniences for your tenants. For example, consider accepting rental payments online. This takes a lot of the risk out for you; tenants don't lose checks in the mail. The transaction can be made through any number of means (credit, debit, PayPal) and it can even be set as an automatic recurring payment from the tenant's bank account so it's easiest for everyone.

Tenants also want modern convenience. Again, it might be beneficial to create a checklist you can use when evaluating any prospective property. In this case, you'll want to investigate details like:
- Nearby shopping and amenities
- Nearby schools and parks
- Public transportation
- High-speed internet and Wi-Fi
- Nearby restaurants and entertainment
- Local tourism, recreation, career growth, and higher education
- New development in the area

Take a look at what the average rental offers and what the high-end rentals offer in your selected location. Find the conveniences that seem to be in highest demand and consider adding those to your offer.

47. What are the electrical regulations for an HMO?

As part of the health and safety legislation, there are electrical regulations an HMO must adhere to. Though you need to check this with the Local Authority for differences, in general the main electrical regulations to watch for and adhere to in the case of your HMO will be:

- Ensuring a qualified electrician provides an onsite walkthrough Electrical Installation Condition Report which can be provided to the council upon request. Your HMO licence will usually expire every five years so perhaps you can line up these two tasks so you can do them together every five years.

- Ensuring all major electrical appliances have safety certificates and this documentation is saved and accessible upon request.

- Plugs and sockets must be part-insulated in order to prevent shock when removing plugs from sockets, and all plugs must be pre-wired.

48. What are the fire safety requirements for an HMO?

The fire and emergency regulations are a bit stricter in an HMO because the living conditions are such that rooms may more frequently be locked between roommates, as they don't necessarily know or interact with one another. As such, the regulations are a bit more stringent. Although I absolutely recommend checking on the exact rules for your selected location, you can generally expect these standard fire and emergency regulations for any HMO:

- Thumb-turn locks on bedroom doors and front and back entrances. This design is meant to be able to be locked and unlocked quickly, and without a key, in an emergency situation. Tenants in an HMO often lock the door to their private sleeping room so it's much safer to employ a lock that can be controlled quickly for emergency exits.

- Fire doors must be installed to ensure that all escape routes can be secured in the event of an emergency or fire.

- Fire alarms should be present in each sleeping room and any corridor.

- A heat-fire alarm should be installed in a shared kitchen.

- Fire extinguishers and fire blankets should be provided with the rental.

- Fire furniture. If you provide furnishings with the rental, it must be with furniture manufactured after 1989 or it will not pass fire inspection.

- Carbon monoxide alarms must be in all rooms that include a solid fuel-burning appliance.

49. What are the gas safety requirements for an HMO?

As an operator of a registered HMO property, you are expected to pay for the inspection of the gas services at the property and then provide certification to the local council of passing that inspection. The inspection must be conducted by only a Competent Person and if the inspection fails, you are expected to rectify the failures and re-inspect for a passing certification.

In most agreements, you are the party responsible for organising, documenting, and submitting the certification for the gas safety requirements, but in some cases, this might be the property owner. Whomever actually takes care of it, I recommend you stay on top of this task being completed each year as part of your regular annual paperwork. If you fail to comply with this law, you run the very real risk of accruing fines due for improper business management, but that's not all. A simple oversight like this could cost you in larger ways. A property could be deemed uninsured at a time it matters most. You may be ordered to cease operation as an HMO immediately, and the property itself could even be seized by the mortgage lenders if this is an infraction on their own terms and agreements.

50.   Do I need planning permission and building approval?

If you're making renovations to a property, you'll probably need building approval, planning permission, or both.

Building approval is sought online when the following work will be done to a property:
- replace fuse boxes and connected electrics
- install a bathroom that will involve plumbing
- change electrics near a bath or shower
- put in a fixed air-conditioning system
- replace windows and doors
- replace roof coverings on pitched and flat roofs
- install or replace a heating system
- add extra radiators to a heating system

Planning permission is a little different and permission should be sought online for larger projects like:

- Demolition to the property
- Building something new
- Making major structural changes to the building
- Changing the use of the building; such as a change from an AST to an HMO.

Chapter 8:
Business Setup and Maintenance

Now it's time to break out and take the lead. In theory, the steps covered in this next section should probably happen before you approach the starting line. By taking these steps first, you'll actually gain an advantage by a faster reaction time at the start of the race, so that when you get to the parts of the rent-to-rent process when an established business is important (especially in the case of an HMO), then you'll already be prepared and you won't have to slow your roll.

In this section, you'll learn the difference between, and benefits of, the various business structures with which to establish your own business. You'll also get a look at other business requirements, like registering your business, registering your property, establishing banking, joining the very necessary authorized redress scheme, and how to account for business tax. Plus, I'll review council tax with you, what it's for, who pays for it, and the consequence of leaving it unpaid. We'll also take a brief look at GDPR compliance and how to ensure you're following the rules.

You're at the top end of the track and you're on the way to a brand-new HMO rental. Don't stop now. You're almost home.

51.   What kind of business structure should I establish?

There are three types of business structures to select from in order to start your small rent-to-rent business. There are advantages and disadvantages to each. It's not uncommon for a business to start with one structure and to grow into another as your success grows.

A sole trader structure is the simplest and fastest to set up, but it carries the most risk. As a sole trader, you're a legal business but under your own personal identity. All business is your personal responsibility to repair with your own financial assets. If another individual, business, or insurance company pursues you legally, it's you personally and there will be no separation between you and your business operation.

A limited company structure allows you to set up your business separately from yourself so that if your business starts to deteriorate, you are not personally responsible for these debts. You may still be responsible to repair these debts, but your personal assets are safe. It's a bit more work at the start but my personal recommendation is that it's well worth it to protect your personal assets. As a limited company, you'll be responsible for keeping formal documentation of company records and for updating any business structure changes you make throughout the year. You'll also be required to file company tax returns and pay corporate taxes.

A partnership structure is the most complex of the three options, but as you might suspect, the available opportunities may be greater for you depending on your circumstances. It's important to note that a partnership does not necessarily mean two (or more) individuals. A partnership can exist between two individuals, an individual and an existing limited company, or two limited companies. A limited company essentially counts as a 'legal person'.

There are also two different types of partnerships from which to select your structure: a limited partnership, and a limited liability partnership. The major difference between these two partnerships is the liability. In a limited partnership, both partners (whether limited company or individual) are personally responsible for debts by the business. However, each partner is personally responsible for debts only up to the amount of which that partner has contributed to the business. In a limited liability partnership, partners are better protected from personal liability.

Partners split profits and pay taxes independently on what they've collected. If you're interested in finding out more about how to select a business structure for your rent-to-rent business, and the requirements that go with each, I recommend my first book *Rent to Rent: A Complete Rental Property Investment Guide* which covers this in greater detail.

52.   How do I establish myself professionally?

If you've chosen to operate as a sole trader, setting up a business banking account is advised but not mandatory. On the other hand, if you've chosen to operate as a limited company or a partnership, a business bank account is required. Here again, is a small lesson to learn from my own mistakes.

Operating as a sole trader out of your own personal bank account might feel nice when the money goes in, but keeping track of your business finances through your own bank account can be a headache. Operating out of your own personal banking account is possibly even a violation according to your bank. There could be a stipulation in your bank's terms and conditions which states that your personal banking account is for personal use only. Just get the business banking account. The cost is very minimal and the setup protects you better, and often comes with a variety of business banking solutions and support that will make your life easier and your business grow faster.

Use QuickBooks for your accounting and record-keeping. QuickBooks makes it simple to manage your business' income and expenses, invoices, taxes, reporting and analytics, receipts, 1099s, bills, and projected profitability. If QuickBooks doesn't sound like the right software for you, there are alternative applications available.

Get yourself a business phone number and a business email address. Both are pretty simple to secure; you just need to make a few choices about how you want this to go. Often times, a rent-to-rent business professional just starting out will use a personal cell phone number and email address. There's nothing wrong with this, but if you're operating as a limited company or partnership, you're going to need official contact information anyway. One thing to think about if you're going to start with the email and phone number you already have, is that now the public essentially has access to your personal number and email address and this can soon become rather annoying. Another detail to consider if you're using your own email address is professionalism. You don't want to be dispensing an email address that looks unprofessional, overly-revealing, or offensive. This is very easily avoided and free to overcome. Create a free and separate email address for your business communications with Gmail, or any other number of email client services. Sometimes when you acquire a website domain and host, you receive a free email account that matches your site. This is the most professional image and my personal favourite choice.

53.   Is it necessary to join the redress scheme?

If you're planning for an HMO operation, then in short, yes, a redress scheme is necessary. If you are hosting lodging accommodations you need not join, but you still can and there are still benefits. The PRS, or Property Redress Scheme, is authorised by the Department for Communities and Local Government and by the National Trading Standards Estate Agency Team to help consumers with complaints and disputes in rental situations. If a complaint or dispute is raised to you from either the property owner or the tenant, you should seek to resolve the issue to your best, and unbiased, ability. Unresolved complaints from either the property owner or the tenant can be raised to the PRS for resolution if none has been found. The PRS acts as an independent and unbiased agency and though the focus is to help the consumer, it's a huge help to you as well. Becoming a member of the PRS shows that your business is dedicated to its service for both your property owners and tenants. It's also a demonstration that you care deeply about improving real estate standards in your area.

Joining is easy and affordable. Submit an application and when your application is accepted, you will pay an annual membership fee of £200 or less, depending on the type of membership you seek. When you've paid, the PRS provides a sticker for display at your place of operation, and leaflets which should be given to your clients; both property owners and tenants upon finalising and closing your contracts with each.

If you fail to join the PRS and a complaint is lodged against you, you risk having to submit and pay anyhow, and on top of that you risk fines. This is another step you *do not* skip if you're operating a respectable and ethical rent-to-rent business.

54. What is the Council Tax and who pays it?

Council tax is a local tax and if you're operating an HMO, chances are it's you who will pay it. However, it's acceptable to build this fee into the cost of rent, as it is truly the residents who benefit from local services, but you will be paying it as the property owner. The fee protects residents in the case of local services and benefits, fire services, and police services. The government contributes a capped amount toward each region and the difference between that and the actual cost to provide these services and is taxed to local residents equally. Council Tax is determined by the worth of the property and falls on a scale that ranges in cost from £996.70 to £2,990.08. Pay the tax when it comes due. Failure to pay your Council Tax revokes your ability to pay in instalments and the total is now due in full, immediately. If you still fail to make this payment, the local council will do what it can to collect these fees from you quickly, including impounding wages and goods in order to make up for the amount owed.

55. What business tax is involved?

If you're establishing a business entity separate from yourself, you'll most probably be responsible for paying a business tax as well. What you pay, and how you do it is determined by the type of business structure you create. Gov.uk does a fantastic job of walking beginners through the business setup process step by step and including taxes.

56. How do I create a business plan?

The answer to this question really depends on why you're creating a business plan. Is it for you? Is it for an investor? Do you need this to be a working document or a formal presentation? There are three common types of business plans: a working plan, an abbreviated plan, and a formal plan.

A working business plan is probably what you need most. This will provide you with a rough internal document to work from and share with others inside the business. It's your business guideline and it's used on a regular basis to steer your ship. This plan is generally very descriptive in order to help you and your staff understand goals, benchmarks, milestones, and deadlines. It's not necessarily the most beautifully formatted document and you'd want to formalise and format it before presenting it in any official capacity.

An abbreviated business plan is more formal and much shorter. If a typical formal plan is about 20 pages in length, an abbreviated plan is about 5 pages (or fewer). This version of your business plan is typically presented to lenders or investors, so it should be a formal copy that's clear and concise.

A formal plan is your full and complete business plan ready for any audience you wish to share it with. This version of your business plan can be as long as 10 or 20 pages and includes all the typical sections of a business plan in detail, including financial records and other formal documentation. This can be used for lenders and investors, but keep in mind that sometimes these parties are more interested in the abbreviated plan.

A 12-month business strategy is more about the planning and less about the plan. Sitting down to write out the sections of a business plan forces you and your staff to think about aspects of your business you may have otherwise overlooked.

Your 12-month business plan is a living document. It changes and grows in order to overcome challenges, obstacles, and shifting goals. It's not a rigid dictation of exactly what must happen, and it's going to be detrimental to stay so rigid.

The major mistake made with a 12-month rent-to-rent business plan is the amount of time and effort put into it. It's often too much or too little time. The level of time and detail you put into it will be affected by whether the document is meant to be presented or used as a working guide, internally. While you certainly want to spend more than a day to create your business plan, you probably don't want to spend more than a month making it or it's taking up too much of your time. When you make your initial 12-month plan, aim for about 5-10 pages in length, unless you're expecting to present a formal document to investors or lenders.

A business plan doesn't necessarily need to follow a certain format, but it should include certain information and sections.

An "executive summary" is typically at the start of the document and it includes a description of your rent-to-rent business; the business concept and the mission statement. This part of the document is meant to give those reading it a general understanding of how the business operates. This typically explains the day-to-day business functions, the location and surrounding environment of the business, and the people involved in performing regular tasks for the business.

A "financial status and strategy" section of the 12-month business plan can vary a bit depending on whether your business is new and just starting or whether you're several years into the business. If you're new, this section typically includes a breakdown of the start-up costs you anticipate, that business capital you currently have or want to establish, usually through a borrowing plan. This section should also include a projected cash flow statement and a profit-and-loss statement. Great plans will also include a break-even analysis that describes how your business plans to at least break even if no significant profit is made over the course of 12 months. This is more important to include if you seek to borrow money and you're presenting this business plan to lenders or investors.

While the "marketing strategy" section is often more significant for businesses selling a product, it's still important to include it, though it doesn't have to be as long as a business plan that includes sold products at a brick-and-mortar location or via eCommerce. In this section, you should include a description of how you plan to market your properties online and/or in the community. This could include any social media marketing plans, Google Ads, the viewing and negotiation process, and even networking strategies, which is definitely part of any successful rent-to-rent business.

The "customer analysis" section of your business plan should include a breakdown of the customer base you intend to serve. Describe your primary customer; your ideal customer; your target customer. If you plan to serve one sort of customer during the start of the year but you plan to expand or shift to another sort of customer within your 12-month period, explain that as well. If you can, describe your customer's median income and what that customer is used to paying for your services in your area.

The "competitor analysis" section should include a profile of the competition and their services, the amount of competition in your region, and the median cost for their services. Describe what the competition does for marketing, the length of time the average competition has been operational in your region, and probably most importantly, how you plan to compete. Find what sets you apart from the competition and makes your services unique. This will often be the number one way you get a leg up on the competition.

Include an "industry analysis". Your audience may not always be familiar with the industry or profession in which you work. Describe to them in this section what the industry profile is. Explain what the industry has looked like in your region over the last 5 years and whether cost and profit have increased or decreased. Include the supply and demand for these industry services and the expected projection for this over the next five years.

Perhaps one of the most important sections for you to complete - for yourself - is a SWOT analysis. A SWOT analysis is a comprehensive study of your business' strengths and weaknesses; your opportunities and threats. Taking time to write up this portion of the business plan is often very revealing and will allow you to spot concerns and opportunities you may not have noticed without performing this bit of work. It's a beneficial section for the audience of your document, but this is almost always more important to the business itself as a planning tool. I highly recommend you concentrate efforts on this section of your 12-month business plan, and perhaps even start here and use what you find to determine other sections of your business strategy.

In the "contingency plan" section of your document, you need to plan for worst-case scenarios. The contingency plan is used to prepare for an outcome that's unlikely, but disastrous if it should occur. Explain why the outcome would be a huge negative impact on your business. Describe how your business plans to mitigate these damages and repair them, should they occur.

Goals and KPIs (Key Performance Indicators) are often a part of each relevant section, but usually a 12-month business plan will dedicate an entire section to defining the milestone goals that will determine your success and growth. KPIs and other metrics are used to measure the success of each goal so that you can tell how much under or over your goal your business has performed. It also serves as an excellent gauge on the timeframe in which each of these goals are accomplished so you can tell if your projected timeframe is over, under, or right on target. Year over year, this part of your plan will serve as a crucial element in your growth. You'll be able to compare last year's goals and KPIs with the goals you set for the coming year.

A 12-month business plan does not necessarily require the inclusion of your "elevator pitch" but this is an excellent exercise and inclusion for new businesses and a beneficial section to add, especially to the working, living, guiding internal business plan. Including a section for your elevator pitch will allow you to focus and refine the explanation of what your business does, in a way that others can understand in about 30 seconds or less.

If you're feeling overwhelmed putting together a 12-month business plan for the first time, don't panic. It will take patience, concentration, and serious logical thought, but it opens you up to a perspective on your business growth that you may have missed without the exercise of making a business plan. Software applications and business plan templates are available online, both for free and for a price, that automate and manage business plans, if that's more your style. If you have the budget for it, there are services that will make your plan for you with your help and then review it with you to make sure you benefit from it as much as your audience will.

It can be a big project for a start-up, but it will be more difficult along the way if you skip this step. The plan for year two will be easier, and then for year three. You'll get the hang of it and your business will keep its momentum on the rails.

57.   How do I ensure I'm GDPR compliant?

GDPR, or the General Data Protection Regulation, is an enormous concept with hundreds, if not thousands, of facets to it. GDPR deals with the protection, processing, storage, and movement of personal information collected through business and commerce.

If you stop for a moment and think about all of the various kinds of business and commerce that take place every day, and all of the possible points in which any personal information is collected, your head starts to spin. Personal information could be a name, a phone number or email address, an IP address, a credit card number; it can even be a business card you collected from someone at a networking event. There are seemingly endless points in a business interaction where personal information is collected. Once the information is collected, it's generally processed in some way and stored somehow, be it in a hardcopy file in your office, or in the digital cloud.

The general idea behind GDPR is for businesses to increase the security and transparency of the personal information they collect. The EU does this by giving the owner of the personal data (the person whose data it is) more control over what happens with their information, and the ability to have that information removed from databases should they no longer wish for the business to possess it.

For you, that means any information you collect from prospects, property owners, tenants, suppliers, employees, or industry colleagues, and what you do with that information after it's collected. This includes how you store it, share it, transmit it, process it, and delete it.

Everything GDPR can be found on the data protection pages of the European Commission, here: https://ec.europa.eu/info/law/law-topic/data-protection_en. The site is remarkably well-managed, current, and easy to use and search. The information on the site comes directly from the European Commission so you can be confident it's accurate and up-to-date information.

Chapter 9:
Marketing Strategy

Maybe you didn't know it but you've had nitrous tanks in the back of this car the whole time. Time to boost your game with super-fuel.

In this case, your super-fuel is a strong and consistent marketing plan for your business. Having this in place is like adding boosters to your rocket.

In this section, let's take a moment to understand exactly how and where to target your audience, what to say, and how to say it.

I'll share with you one of my absolute favourite direct mail marketing techniques that takes a little time upfront, but works like magic on property owners. Because most of the world's attention and commerce lives online today, I'll also go over a few online marketing strategies worth your consideration. Having nitrous bumps you up a class in the race, and sends you streaking toward the finish of a profitable rental property.

58.   How do I find and target my audience?

We've talked briefly about marketing to an audience of either property owners or tenants, but now let's break it down. There are two major locations you'll find your audience, whoever they may be: online and offline, and by offline, I mean real life. I separate them this way because there are so many ways to market both online and offline, and they no doubt have their own unique tactics and approaches. In either case, the goal is to find out where your prospects go, go there, and get in front of them with a compelling offer.

Let's start online and for the sake of example, let's say your property model is an HMO. When you go online, you'll be seeking property owners with available HMO-style dwellings, and tenants to fill the unit. Where do property owners (and their property postings) go, online? Where do target tenants go, online? Sometimes, these audiences can even be found in the same places. For example, both property owners and prospective tenants will visit local networking sites like Gumtree or Nextdoor in addition to local Facebook groups. Visit these and other local network sites. Here, you can find properties being rented out that would make for a perfect HMO and approach the property owners with your offer via email, online post, or messenger.

Side note when it comes to marketing online or off, record what you do and do one audience at a time. For example, I keep a simple Excel document for my own prospecting. I keep track of when I contact someone, who, how, what I offer, and any response or follow-up notes that are important for me to track. Additionally, I've come to find it useful in tracking demographic information on these opportunities, too. Recording your prospecting process will help you keep track of all you do in the short-term, but this information you record reveals patterns over time which can make you an even sharper rent-to-rent business person.

On the same type of local networking sites, you'll be able to find prospective tenants. Once you've lined up your property for subletting, publish the listing online. It's worth mentioning again that the pictures you take and publish of the property will be an important marketing factor. Take well-angled, well-lit photos of all the interior space and exterior space. Take pictures of each room or area the tenant will have access to, and even from multiple angles. It's better to have too many pictures than too few. It's very common that rental postings that do not include photos get skipped and overlooked from the start. Give your tenant audience the ability to visualise themselves in your property. In addition to great photos, provide an enticing description of the property, and the expectations that come with it, such as the cost of rent, the HMO-style accommodations, and anything worth highlighting. With these basic steps, tenants find you.

That's just the beginning of online marketing opportunities. Depending on your online presence, you could have a website of managed and available properties, and online application process, a blog, online discounts, and social media accounts. You can join groups for professionals on LinkedIn or Facebook to network with the audience you seek. These ideas are free or low-cost, but if you have a small amount of money (say £100 or so) to invest, you can even run Facebook ad campaigns to make sure prospective tenants see your available listing. Want to go even further? Consider running Google Ad campaigns to target a fuller, yet more specific audience. This can cost upwards of about £1000 to get started, but the leads you gather are generally highly qualified opportunities.

Keep going and join or register with online trade associations or websites used by estate agents. This can help you get in front of the property owner-side of marketing for your business and build a trusted and authoritative presence locally. You can find these groups on just about any social media platform. You might also try Citizens Advice and Trading Standards, which are authorised organisations that help consumers find trustworthy landlords (among other things).

Now turn off your computer and step outside. You're in a whole other world of marketing potentials. Walk or drive around the neighbourhoods of your selected location and find places with signs for rent and collect the phone numbers or call on the spot to introduce yourself to the property owners. Wander into a few local agency offices and make friends with the competition. In my experience, I've found that we aren't really competitors, but colleagues. There's more than enough business to go around and we're all targeting our own niches. It's so much more common for me to pass opportunities to other agents and property managers that don't quite fit me but do fit them, than it is to compete for clients or tenants.

Create a direct marketing campaign by collecting the phone numbers and/or addresses of property owners and businesses that would be interested to know about your business and your offer. Don't get tunnel vision here. It's not just other real estate professionals you want to expose your offer to, it's businesses on the periphery, as well. This might be contractors and service providers you might do business with in the future, or businesses that would be interested in prospecting to you.

Two very common offline contact methods are via direct phone marketing and direct mail marketing. In either case, your approach can be a friendly introduction and perhaps some kind of free offer of value. That offer can really be anything that is relevant and useful to your audience. It might be a tool, an article, a coupon, or offers from other local businesses you've partnered with for an ad campaign.

Another real-world marketing method I love is networking events. This is an audience ready and willing to know what you do and how you can be mutually helpful to one another. Put on your business best and polish your marketing materials and business cards. Practice your elevator pitch.

It might take some creativity and some practice to find the marketing methods, online and offline that work best for your business, but once you find your favourites, you can fine-tune the approach and apply the same campaigns in nearly any area you choose.

59. What do I say and how do I say it?

What to say and how to say it is much the same as when you're negotiating; you want to be honest and transparent about your vision and your offer, and you want to deliver it in a compelling way. Include an offer to entice your audience, and give them directions for what to do next- this is the call to action. An example might be offering tenants a free rental application process when they apply on your website.

If you're talking to property owners, highlight the idea of guaranteed rent and cost-free property management. If you're talking to prospective tenants, highlight all the awesome features of the property.

Regardless of your audience, you want to create a sense of urgency when talking to them. This can be indirectly or with more formality; whichever works better for you. Give some indication from the beginning that you're working expeditiously to meet your goal, be it signing to the management of a property or settling the tenancy sublet agreements.

60.   How do I create and send a direct mail leaflet?

When I enter a new location, I collect the addresses of the properties that are available for rent - or even better, should be available but are just sitting unused, and send them direct mail marketing. Relatives sometimes inherit property, and they aren't sure whether to sell it or rent it out so it sits vacant for a while. In other cases, the property owner has been busy with other pieces of life and just doesn't have time to manage a property or even rent it out. They don't really want the hassle of managing such a project but they do like the idea of passive income. Enter you with the solution.

One of the most successful direct mail campaigns I've done, and continue to do, is the newsletter campaign.

For about £10, I outsourced a designer on Fiverr to create a 6-page newsletter template that I end up using every new location I work in.

The newsletter looks like an official estate agent's publication and I substitute local details in each place I go so that it looks authentic. This might be the names of local towns, businesses, landmarks, or recent events. On the front of the newsletter and under the title I feature an attractive picture of the owner's property. This is an immediate eye-catcher for any owner. They will immediately be curious about why their property is featured on the cover of this newsletter and about how they didn't know.

Now I drop some compelling article headlines on the front cover, like:
- See how owner, {Name}, increased property revenue by 86% in one year
- Property highlights of {Street Address}
- The benefits of subletting as an HMO in {City Name}
- How the guaranteed rent plan saved my family home in {City Name}

...and really any other points I want to set in the mind of the reader. £10 to £1, that property owner is definitely going to open that newsletter and read on. As they do, they'll pick up the key points in your offer; the key attractors; the primary ideas you want to convey. As they read, they will probably realise the document is a piece of marketing material, but at that point it won't matter because the ideas will have sunk in. Don't lie in the document, but rather, report on the success you could offer to the property owner if he or she were to partner with you. Highlight the pain-points of trying to rent out and manage your own property and then suggest a property manager like yourself and the solutions you offer. The articles can be the same for any prospective property owner, with a few substitutions to make it relevant, local, and customized. Absolutely include a call to action and a way to contact you.

61.   How do I create an email marketing campaign?

Take everything I've explained about the direct mail newsletter campaign, make a digital version of the newsletter, and send it in an email. That's it.

Well, it's not completely it. Rather than collect physical addresses you'll want to collect email addresses. Rather than relying on just the newsletter headlines, you'll need to create a catchy subject line for the email.

Remember that for email marketing, you have a bit more control over how and when the information is received by your audience. For example, you can choose to send your marketing email on a day you suspect property owners will be paying closer attention to email, like Saturdays and Mondays, or perhaps at a certain time in the day, like 9 o'clock at night.

62.   How do I create other online ad campaigns?

There are a number of popular methods of advertising online; email marketing and promoting your own website is just the beginning. Online ad campaigns are designed to direct more traffic to your site, landing pages, or sales pages with the intent and hope that the visitor follows the call to action.

If you do have some kind of website or business presence online, you may want to consider an SEO campaign. SEO stands for search-engine-optimization. To oversimplify, it's the practice of using strategically selected and placed keywords in your web content in order to drive your pages up when those keywords are searched. This traffic is organic; that is to say, it comes to your site or pages without you paying for it.

PPC, or pay-per-click, is like an SEO campaign, but also a bit like the stock market, in that you're paying for keywords, so you can hold one of the first several positions on Google when those keywords are searched. This deliberately drives a high amount of traffic to your site and increases the leads and sales you make.

Social media campaigns are similar marketing methods, but they're set up on social media platforms like Facebook, LinkedIn, or Instagram.

If you have the resources to invest in online advertising, I highly recommend hiring a PPC agency to help you out. Whether you advertise with Google Ads or a social media platform like Facebook, it can be a lot of work and a full-time job unto itself. Pony-up the extra money and hire a manager for the best return on investment.

If you want to do it yourself, there's a lot to learn, but it's possible. You can become a Google Ads partner and manage your own campaigns, and social media campaigns have easy-to-use interfaces to set your campaign and target your audience.

Chapter 10:

Business Growth

This section on business growth and development is likened to becoming a better race car driver. You've already got the tools. You've developed the skills. You've collected the knowledge. Now it's about honing your craft; it's about sharpening your expertise.

Let's assume you've done well at the races and it's time to expand. In this section, we'll take a look at what to expect for a reasonable ROI in your first year, and thereafter.

I'll share with you the next steps to growing your business on a local and digital level. I'll explain when and how I rely on outsourcers and contractors to get my work done quickly and efficiently. This leaves me more time for the harder decisions that require my input.

I'll also give you some ideas on how to advance yourself personally and professionally in a way that will be beneficial to your real estate growth. Position yourself as an authority and create the image of a local go-to professional when it comes to rentals and real estate. You've made it to the final section of this book. Did you think you'd approach the finish line with the momentum and confidence as you now have?

63.   What kind of ROI can I expect in my first year?

The kind of ROI (Return on Investment) you can expect in your first year, and thereafter, is an answer which is very similar to how fast you can make a profit. It depends on the situation; specifically, your expenses and your income in a given situation. In your first year, you'll have business start-up expenses, renovations, updates, and maintenance costs. You may have a council tax, utility expenses, marketing expenses. You might need to pay for business insurance, redress scheme membership, taxes, and various minor business expenses. If your business has employees, you'll definitely need to consider taxes and employee rights and benefits, even in the case of freelance contractors in some cases.

What you get as an ROI varies. However, as a benchmark, you can assume a good return on investment is about 10-12%, and you're doing really well at 15%. This might not be an achievable number for you in the first year due to all the beginning expenses, but find out how many years it will take to reach that kind of goal.

64.   What are the next steps to grow my business?

Analysing the top 20% of your customers; create customer profiles of them. Identify who makes up your top 20% of owners, and likewise for your tenants. By analysing, you'll be able to better pinpoint what makes up your best audience and what makes up the other 80%. Target the individuals that make up that top 20% by advertising in places they will see.

Offer value they seek. Set higher costs that are still affordable.

Consider listing your business and/or your available properties on directories like:

- Google My Business
- Spareroom
- Facebook
- Instagram
- Twitter
- Gumtree
- Bing Places
- 118Information
- ThePhoneBook

Collect testimonials and references from happy property owners and tenants you've worked with. Ask these individuals to provide a written testimonial to either be given to you for use as you see fit, or online in any of the relevant directories that offer ratings and endorsements. If you have a business website or a social media page, add these testimonials to your site to increase your image as an authority and trusted local resource.

Speaking of which, if you don't have much in the way of an online presence, it's time to change that. Creating a professional business website is easy if you know how and have time, but if you don't, freelancers on sites like Fiverr will do it for you. Creating an entire website when you don't have all that much to say yet can be a big project. If you choose to create a presence for your business using a social media platform (or several), this cuts the cost significantly. You won't need to acquire a domain or hosting, but still, your presence can look very professional. Whichever option you go with, having an online presence in today's world is almost a necessity, especially if you plan to market online. A web presence builds a rapport and sense of ease and trust with your prospects and clients.

If you already have a web presence, it's time to tune it up. Keep them fresh and relevant and refine the locations and audience members you target. Business websites often have opt-in marketing that allows visitors of the site to sign up for newsletters, blogs, and valuable downloadable content. Consider adding or improving these opt-in options and repositioning them on the page for greater visibility and engagement. Sidebars, headers, footers, and banners at the top or bottom of a specific piece of content can work very well. In addition to opt-in options, a business website, landing page, or social media page often includes at least one call-to-action (CTA). A call to action is an enticing offer that pulls interested parties into your sales circle. For example, you might offer an online tenant application that reduces or eliminates the application fee. This offer can pull in prospective tenants so you have less work to do in the hunt for them.
 If you can afford it, hire a freelance digital marketing pro for their expertise.

Have you ever wanted to send your voice out on the airwaves? Run your ad by securing a small slot of time on the local radio for exposure. Radio advertisements can be more cost-effective than print ads, and it will reach a wider audience. This may not target your refined 20%, but you never know who's listening and how they're connected to your next opportunity.

65.   How can I automate work?

Assume first that there is likely a program or application in existence today that does the thing you need to do automatically. For example, let's say you've made an excellent email marketing campaign using the newsletter method. You need that campaign to be emailed to the property owners on a certain date and time, and then you need three additional reminder emails to go out to the property owners through the month which increases the sense of urgency on your offers. You also need a certain response to be sent back to any interested property owner that contacts you in the interim. You don't have time to manage any of this. Luckily a robot can do it for you. Use an email campaign tool (there are plenty of professional enough options both free and paid) to manage all of this for you. Set it once, and let the computer do the rest and fill in the customization where you want it. Just like an email campaign management robot that does it for you, there are automated apps to do almost anything, and many are free. If you find yourself saying, "I don't have time for this", consider if the activity can be automated.

66.   How can I outsource work?

In some cases you'll find yourself saying, "I don't have time for this", and the activity cannot be automated. It takes human engagement to complete the process. There's still a solution that saves you time. If there's not a robot for it, there's a freelance contractor for it. Get someone else to learn your process and repeat it for the activities that need human engagement.

An answering service might seem like a silly or unnecessary expense, but as you become busier with work, it will sound like answers to prayers. These services are affordable; as low as £25/month. If your rent-to-rent business is a side business, an answering service makes even more sense. If prospects and clients call while you're at your other job, a professional is there to answer the call. When prospects and clients call for information and help, they may not get the answer they need, but hearing someone on the other end of the phone, as opposed to a voicemail message, instils a greater deal of confidence in you and your business and it cultivates a feeling of being taken care of. Answering services usually offer a variety of features, like a live, 24/7 receptionist. As you grow, these services can scale with you to support your evolving needs.

67. When is it time to hire contractors and employees?

When you have a team that you can delegate to, the process goes faster and so does the progress. You can acquire more properties and tenants at a greater rate. Imagine if you could pass the more time-consuming tasks to others you could trust. Imagine if you could pay someone else to run your marketing, conduct your viewings, run background checks, and draw up the paperwork? You'll suddenly find your schedule open for the heavier business decisions and developments. It's time to start bringing on other team members when you can afford it financially, but no longer in time. Start slow with one new team member at a time if it suits you, or if you can afford it, arm yourself with an entire team at once.

63. How should I continue to grow as an authority of rent-to-rent?

Take time to write a blog or a feature article in a local print. A consistent online publication can quickly help to establish you as an experienced professional and authority in the industry. If you don't have the time to keep up with a blog or write an online feature article, consider hosting an online AMA (Ask Me Anything) and inviting interested members of your target audience to participate, such as one event for tenants and one for property owners and peripheral business professionals. You could also create a profile on sites like Business.com and Quora and find questions that pertain to your industry and answer them.

Search your selected area for local events that your business can volunteer for. These events don't need to be industry-related and often work better when they aren't. If you can't attend or participate, you can sponsor someone within the community. You expose yourself to the community and your involvement will get your business noticed.

Another tip for continued growth is to stay fresh and learn new practices, new techniques, and updated regulations in the world of rent-to-rent. There will always be new and changing information to keep up with if you are to be an authority in your field.

Online, you can find courses, seminars, and webinars that will develop your understanding of rent-to-rent business further. Many courses can be taken online and at your own pace. Live courses in your local area are often available multiple times a year. This might suit you better than an online learning environment. An option like this educates you and provides an exclusive networking circle for you with local professionals.

To get help on a more personal level, consider seeking out a coach or mentor to work with you one-on-one, with your specific business plan. It's true that a coach or mentor will likely only support you for a fee, but this is well worth the cost. There's nothing quite as reassuring as checking your decision against someone trustworthy who has already been through it and learned.

Conclusion

You made it over the finish line! Congratulations! You've completed *Rent to Rent: You've Got Questions, I've Got Answers!*

Not only are you fully prepared to find and manage your own rent-to-rent enterprise, you probably also understand how to race your dragster over the line.

It has been an exciting and rewarding journey to guide you in your rent-to-rent travels. As you've been in the passenger's seat, you've been collecting a wealth of crucial information. You've seen examples, heard stories, witnessed consequences and wins. You know what it takes to establish a professional and ethical rent-to-rent business and how to operate in full accordance with laws and regulations.

Now it's time for us to switch seats. You take the wheel. I'll be your ride or die for a while. You hit the accelerator. You steer. I'm sure you have what it takes. You've quenched that insatiable thirst to know how others are making a profitable living from rent-to-rent investments. You've invested the time. Your creative genius is piqued. You've demonstrated your adaptability and resilience. Because of this, the prize just over the finish line for which you were so passionate; it's yours.

It's my genuine hope that throughout the pages of this book, you've picked up the skills and knowledge it takes to crack the rent-to-rent code. I'm truly looking forward to seeing you on the other side of the finish line; HMO trophies in hand and winnings spilling from your pockets.

In no time at all you've gone from 0 to 60 like a professional. You're already miles ahead of most of the rent-to-rent race cars out there. I'm excited and proud to see where you'll take this next.

From this point on, you can roll into the world of rent-to-rent investment with the confidence of a drag racer. Some don't have what it takes, or they never learn, or they never have the passion. Not you. Drive and determination is all it takes. Skills and knowledge are at your command. The only thing standing between you and success is a strip of track that I'm confident you can clear. Put your car on the tracks. Drive it like you stole it, and there's no going back.

A Short message from the Author:

Hey, did you enjoy reading this book? I'd love to hear your thoughts!

Many readers do not know how hard reviews are to come by, and how much they help a new author like myself. Reviews alone are what typically makes my book stand out in the crowd and persuades another person to choose this book.

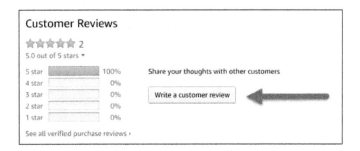

I would be incredibly grateful if you could take just 60 seconds is all it takes to write a brief review (even if it's just a few sentences) on whatever bookstore or marketplace you purchased this book from!

Thank you for taking the time to share your thoughts!

Printed in Great Britain
by Amazon

84941676R00150